Elizabeth Bishop's
World War II–Cold War View

Courtesy of the Library of Congress.

Elizabeth Bishop's
World War II–Cold War View

Camille Roman

palgrave

ELIZABETH BISHOP'S WORLD WAR II–COLD WAR VIEW
Copyright © Camille Roman, 2001.

First published 2001 by
PALGRAVE™
175 Fifth Avenue, New York, N.Y. 10010 and
Houndmills, Basingstoke, Hampshire, England RG21 6XS.
Companies and representatives throughout the world.

PALGRAVE™ is the new global publishing imprint of St. Martin's Press LLC Scholarly and Reference Division and Palgrave Publishers Ltd (formerly Macmillan Press Ltd).

ISBN 0-312-23078-8 hardback

Library of Congress Cataloging-in-Publication Data
Roman, Camille, 1948-
  Elizabeth Bishop's World War II-Cold War view / Camille Roman.
    p. cm.
  Includes bibliographical references and index.
  ISBN 0-312-23078-8
  1. Bishop, Elizabeth, 1911-1979—Political and social views. 2. Politics and literature—United States—History—20th century. 3. Political poetry, American—History and criticism. 4. World War, 1939-1945—Literature and the war. 5. Cold War in literature. 6. War in literature. I. Title.
  PS3503.I785 Z85 2000
  811'.54—dc21   00-055689

A catalogue record for this book is available from the British Library.

Design by Westchester Book Composition

First edition: January 2001
10 9 8 7 6 5 4 3 2 1

Printed in the United States of America.

For Chris Darwin Frigon

No art without life; no life without art.
—*Theodor Leschetizky*

Contents ⌐

Acknowledgments

This book would not have been possible without the collective enterprise of the many scholars, historians, poets, writers, critics, artists, and journalists cited throughout its pages and in the bibliography. I owe an immeasurable debt to them as well as to countless others whom I have not been able to cite fully but who also gave generously to this project. To all, then, from whom I have learned about Elizabeth Bishop and the World War II–Cold War victory culture, I express my deepest appreciation.

Bishop's friend, the late poet James Merrill, whom I met at his reading at Brown University in the fall of 1990, encouraged my work during that meeting. When he learned that I had written about both Bishop and him in my dissertation, his face and eyes lit up with vivid pleasure. He spoke with such warmth about her that this memory, for which I am deeply grateful, has been like a companion during this project.

Alice Quinn, poetry editor of *The New Yorker*, took time at the 1998 Worcester Conference on Bishop to discuss the August 19, 1996 issue of the magazine featuring a Garry Wills piece on John Wayne and "Easel by Elizabeth Bishop," a collage of poetry and art. I am most grateful for her openness and curiosity about my response to the juxtaposition of Wayne and Bishop, which I wrote into this project.

My first encounter with Bishop's poem "Visits to St. Elizabeths" in Mutlu Blasing's graduate seminar on post–1945 American poetry at Brown University ignited questions that led to this book. I wrote my dissertation, which included a chapter on Bishop's poetry, under Blasing's direction with committee members George Monteiro and Susanne Woods at Brown University and Patricia Yaeger at Harvard University. This was an incomparable opportunity for exploring Bishop's poetry for the first time with four distinguished scholars who taught and wrote on Bishop themselves. I am deeply grateful for their support then—and as my work has developed.

Several valuable guides helped me to consider how to interpret Bishop's dialogue with World War II–Cold War culture. I thank my coparticipants in the 1991-92 seminar at the Pembroke Center for Teaching and Research on Women at Brown University as well as my coeditors Suzanne Juhasz and Cristanne Miller on *The Women & Language Debate: A Sourcebook* and such contributors to this volume as Julia Kristéva, Hélène Cixous, Luce Irigaray, Hortense Spillers, Gayatri Spivak, Susan Gal, Nancy Henley, Cheris Kramarae, Penelope Eckert, and Sally McConnell-Ginet. They introduced me to the complexities of gender studies, literary theory, and cultural studies, an invaluable contribution to my thinking.

As I worked on this book, I was invited to read portions of various chapters at conferences. I thank Susan Belasco Smith and Alfred Bendixen of the 1996 American Literature Association Conference; Burton Hatlen of the 1996 Poetry in the 1950s Conference; Laura Menides and Angela Dorenkamp of the 1997 Elizabeth Bishop Conference; Thomas Travisano of the Elizabeth Bishop Society's 1998 American Literature Association sessions; and Sandra Barry, Gwen Davies, and Peter Sanger of the 1998 Nova Scotia Symposium on Elizabeth Bishop for these opportunities. I also thank the MLA 1998 program committee for approving my special session proposal on World War II–Cold War poetic narratives, which featured my paper on Bishop with papers by Steven Gould Axelrod and Lorrie Goldensohn. All of these invaluable forums led to important exchanges that contributed significantly to the development of this book. In addition, I thank Cheryl Walker, Sylvia Henneberg, and Neil Besner for their supportive reviews of several of these conference papers in *The Elizabeth Bishop Bulletin*.

I am grateful to *WLA: War, Literature & the Arts* associate editor David Boxwell for inviting me to contribute an essay on Bishop and the World War II–Cold War narrative to the journal and then to help plan the special 1999 issue on Bishop and the Middle Generation of Poets on War. I thank contributors Steven Gould Axelrod, Lorrie Goldensohn, Thomas Travisano, Gary Fountain, Sandra Barry, and George Monteiro for their essays, some of which are cited in this book.

I also am thankful to Laura Menides and Angela Dorenkamp as well as Sandra Barry, Gwen Davies, and Peter Sanger for the opportunities to publish early versions of parts of this book in *'In Worcester, Massachusetts': Essays on Elizabeth Bishop* and *Division of the Heart: Elizabeth Bishop's Art of Place and Memory.*

This study benefited greatly from Thomas Travisano's and Steven Gould Axelrod's careful readings of earlier drafts in their entirety. I am deeply appreciative of their generous sharing of their own scholarship and invaluable suggestions to improve the manuscript.

I thank the late Margaret Dickie and Sian Hunter White, her editor at the University of North Carolina Press, for early access to her book *Stein, Bishop, Rich* while I was completing the first draft of this project.

Archival and library work was very important to the development of my book. I am very grateful for the professional acumen of Nancy Mac-Kechnie, Curator of Rare Books and Manuscripts, Vassar College, which houses the Bishop and Edna St. Vincent Millay archives. Barbara Page graciously welcomed me at Vassar, for which I am appreciative. I also thank Jennifer Rutland, Poetry & Literature Division, Library of Congress; the John Hay Library, Brown University; and Washington State University Libraries.

For their assistance in locating and reproducing the cover and frontispiece photo of Bishop in her poetry consultancy office at the Library of Congress as well as helping me to include three additional photos of Bishop that I discovered, I thank Helen Dalryple of Public Affairs and Eva Shade of the Photoduplication Service at the Library.

For financial, institutional, and staff support, I wish to thank Brown University and my home institution, Washington State University. My work has benefited greatly from the Jean Starr Untermeyer Poetry Fellowship and appointments as Visiting Scholar in 1996-97 and 1998-2000 in the Department of English at Brown. I am grateful to department chairs Nancy Armstrong, Geoffrey Russom, Stephen Foley, and William Keach for their support of my work as a visiting scholar. I thank Marilyn Netter and Lorraine Mazza of the English department staff for making my visits run smoothly. For sharing their homes with me and supporting me with their friendship, I am deeply grateful to Ruth Oppenheim and Harold Reissner; Tori Smith, Jay Glasson, and Adrian Glasson; and Dorothy Denniston. I also am very appreciative of the collegiality and friendship of Mutlu Blasing, Flora Keshkegian, George Monteiro, Mark and Shelly Spilka, and Susanne Woods.

I wish to express my deep gratitude to Washington State University for a year of sabbatical leave in 1999-2000 and an earlier leave in 1996-97; for research initiation and completion grants from Barbara Couture and John Pierce, Deans of the College of Liberal Arts, 1996-98; for Arts and

Humanities Travel Grants, 1994–96; and for conference funding and course release for research, 1994–99, from the Department of English. I especially thank my department chairs Susan McLeod, Mary Wack, and Victor Villanueva for their support. The Humanities Research Center and Rhonda Blair provided timely assistance. I am grateful to my colleagues and friends at the university for their collegiality and encouragement. My undergraduate and graduate students asked stimulating questions as I developed this book. I thank Ann Ciasullo for being a competent research assistant.

I am grateful to Martha Gregory, formerly of the Lewis & Clark College administration, Portland, Oregon, for introducing me to the tranquil library where much of the first draft was written; and to Patricia O'Brien, for providing editorial support in the final stages of the book.

To Kristi Long, my editor at Palgrave, I express deep appreciation for her enthusiasm, her counsel, her understanding, and her professionalism. I am grateful to the staff at Palgrave for their dedication and support, especially Annjeanette Kern, as well as Karin Cholak, Rick Delaney, Meredith Howard, Amy McDermott, Gabriella Pearce, and Sarah Schur, and to my copyeditor, Enid Stubin.

I wish to thank Caroline Ackerman, Roger Allen, Denise Baer, Ron Beaver, Kimberly Berg, Fanchon Burke, Daria Donaldson, Elizabeth Farregher, Laura Glenn, Martha Gregory, Janet Hansen-Tracy, Ruell Hemphill, Barbara Higgins, Andi John, Freddi Lipstein, Eleanor Lowry, Rajamma Matheu, Patricia O'Brien, Annette O'Donnell, Peter Papulis, Virginia Perry, Alison Reeves, Julie Richie, Richard Romiti, and Jerry Whitmore for their sustaining friendship during this project. I am grateful to my family for their cherished support and friendship, especially Cheryll Faust and Hillard Howard; Betsy and Bob Roman; June and Jim May; and Marion Emerson.

This book is dedicated to my husband Chris Darwin Frigon, who has inspired me with his artistic and intellectual companionship.

Camille Roman

I regret that contract restrictions relating to the pending publication of Bishop's uncollected and unpublished poems made it impossible for me to quote directly from the following: "V-Day August 14th, 1945," two drafts of "View of the Capitol from the Library of Congress," and "Desk at Night."

Excerpts from unpublished writings of Elizabeth Bishop. Reprinted by permission of Farrar, Straus and Giroux, LLC, on behalf of the Estate of Elizabeth Bishop. Copyright © 2000 by Alice Helen Methfessel.

Reprinted by permission of Farrar, Straus and Giroux, LLC:

Approx. 112 lines from THE COMPLETE POEMS 1927-1979 by Elizabeth Bishop. Copyright © 1979, 1983 by Alice Helen Methfessel.

Approx. 167 words from "The Country Mouse" from THE COLLECTED PROSE by Elizabeth Bishop. Copyright © 1984 by Alice Helen Methfessel.

Approx. 616 words from ONE ART by Elizabeth Bishop, selected and edited by Robert Giroux. Copyright © 1994 by Alice Methfessel.

The four photos of Elizabeth Bishop in her poetry consultancy office at the Library of Congress are reprinted courtesy of the Library of Congress.

Excerpts from previously unpublished writings by Elizabeth Bishop and her letters to Pearl Kazin Bell, Ferris Greenslet, and Lloyd Frankenberg are reprinted by permission of Elizabeth Bishop Papers, Special Collections, Vassar College Libraries, Poughkeepsie, New York.

Excerpts from the letters of Elizabeth Bishop to Marianne Moore are reprinted by permission of the Rosenbach Museum and Library.

Portions of chapter 6 appeared, in substantially earlier and altered form, in *In Worcester, Massachusetts: Essays on Elizabeth Bishop from the 1997 Elizabeth Bishop Conference at WPI*, Peter Lang, 1999. © Peter Lang Publishing Inc., New York, 1999, and *Division of the Heart: Elizabeth Bishop's Art of Place and Memory*, Wolfville, Nova Scotia: Gaspereou Press, 2000. Reprinted by permission.

Chapter 1 ～

INTRODUCTION: BISHOP'S WORLD WAR II– COLD WAR VIEW

A professional and poised 38–year-old Elizabeth Bishop leans over her desk at the Library of Congress with a view through her long picture window of the U.S. Capitol in Washington, D.C., in the cover and frontispiece photo. With fountain pen in hand, she seems preoccupied with the papers before her. In our contemporary culture, in which we speak of writers' cultural currency and capital, Bishop appears to have "arrived" in this photo. She was holding the nation's most prestigious position for its poets—the national poetry chair, now known as the poet laureateship, at the Library of Congress, from the fall of 1949 to the fall of 1950. What did she ponder at her desk whenever she looked out the window at the Capitol, where the government was constructing the country's World War II–Cold War domestic and international narrative and leading the nation into the Korean War in 1950?

This book answers the question by telling the story of Bishop's unexplored dialogue with the U.S. victory culture that she brought to her life and writing in Brazil in 1951. In the years immediately following the Second World War, the majority of midcentury Americans agreed that the war had been a "just war" in which the nation emerged triumphant so it became the war story that Cold War policymakers relied upon to narrate the emerging postwar narrative against Communism. Even during the Vietnam conflict in the late 1960s, as Tom Engelhardt has argued persuasively, "the immediate war story within which Americans, from the president on down, still generally cared to live was that of World War II" (11). But not everyone, including Bishop, agreed upon the same version of the Second World War story or upon the various politically driven Cold War appropriations of it. This cultural narrative about Bishop considers her

World War II dialogue to be an integral part of understanding her conversation with Cold War culture. It reveals, for instance, that Bishop was remarkably prescient about the Korean War as a haunting historical turning point in the country's Cold War narrative, installing militarism as a central fact of American civilian life, while most Americans failed to understand and follow the war and promptly forgot about it, preferring to focus on the victory war story of the Second World War.

Narratives like this book about Bishop are by nature question-driven or thesis-driven, because critics and biographers must discover at least one coherent story to tell from the frequently contradictory and confusing multiplicity of a writer's life and writing, not to mention the frustrating gaps, puzzling fragments, and questions. I struggled, often in agony, with Bishop's political decisions and personal choices. The process of discovering and reconstructing the story for the reader is, then, a highly subjective matter. I hope to offer one multinarrative version of the World War II– Cold War dialogue in Bishop's life and writing out of many possible stories, mindful that many more narrators will follow me with important new questions, discoveries, and interpretations. My goal is not to provide an authoritative, comprehensive, or exhaustive view of this period of her life so much as to suggest an "entry" into it.

The official-looking Bishop in her poetry office at the Library of Congress, for instance, looks neither sickly nor mute to my eye with her well-groomed appearance and pen in hand. Indeed she completed important work at the library, arranging for Dylan Thomas to read and recording poets like Robert Frost, Archibald MacLeish, and Muriel Rukeyser.

But she was both ill and reticent. She did not give a public reading while she was poetry consultant. Bishop was struggling with many other conflicts and demands: her poetic genius; an attachment to a protected, privileged life; professional ambition; compromised attempts at recognizing social difference; childhood war trauma; the childhood death of her father and the mental institutionalization of her mother; anxieties about authoritarianism, militarism, Communism, and Fascism; political and historical naïveté and innocence; and lesbianism. The photo taken in Bishop's office as Cold War Communist fear and homophobia took center stage in congressional sessions in the Capitol outside her window does not even hint at these "stories."

Bishop's friend Randall Jarrell once commented perceptively that all of her poems "have written underneath, *I have seen it*" (235). His appraisal is especially accurate for Bishop's World War II–early Cold War writing as she revises the role of women's field of vision in war. Bishop often reported about her life and writing during war. Looking out from a window at the scene before her being transformed into a war landscape, she was aware of her front-row seat in the military theater. She had eyewitness views at the writing study window overlooking Key West Harbor during the Second World War; at a Key West bedroom window watching the arrival of battle in "Roosters"; at a windowsill observing celebrations of V-Day 1945; at a window viewing the Capitol from her poetry office at the Library of Congress in Cold War Washington; at her apartment in San Francisco during the Vietnam War.

Susan Schweik has demonstrated that the conventional history of Western war situates women at one remove and in distress (241). She contends correctly that Bishop foregrounds the role of the "guilty observer" in the World War II–era poem, "Roosters" (249). This book's treatment of Bishop adds new perspectives to the role of the "observer," revealing as well the problems of reluctant, unwilling, forced, colonial, and imperialist "observers" in war. Moreover, in addition to her concerns about eyewitnessing in war, Bishop also focuses on its companion activity—storytelling—in a world of modern air warfare in which boundaries between civilians and the military have collapsed. Everyone is implicated in war, including the surviving observers, storytellers, listeners, and readers.

This narrative about the World War II–Cold War chapter in Bishop's life and writing was made possible by the many illuminating critics and biographers who have gone before me, helping me to probe the curious contradictory silence surrounding Bishop's most highly public year in her poetry career. The major conventional stories of Bishop's life at this time in Margaret Dickie's *Stein, Bishop, Rich,* Gary Fountain's interview-based biography, and Brett Millier's document-based biography offered evidence of Bishop's illness and repression. Dickie, Fountain, and Millier, along with such critics as Steven Axelrod, Jacqueline Brogan, Sandra Gilbert, Lorrie Goldensohn, Susan Gubar, Susan Schweik, and Thomas Travisano, provided strong evidence for the importance of Bishop's poetry about U.S. militarism in the Second World War and the late Cold War. Recent book-length critical studies by Bonnie Costello, Joanne Feit Diehl, Betsy Erkkila, Lorrie Goldensohn, Victoria Harrison, Marilyn May Lombardi, Susan McCabe, and Thomas Travisano established a critical understanding of a public Bishop as well as a private Bishop, thereby indicating a complex narrative at work throughout her life and writing.

Studies of Bishop's long-acknowledged confounding, contradictory, and subversive rhetoric provided resources for understanding her World War II–Cold War strategies. In his essay, "The Elizabeth Bishop Phenomenon,"

Travisano points to such germinal work as "Adrienne Rich's reading of Bishop as an 'outsider,' Lee Edelman's reading of a poet who 'rips the fabric of the cultural text,' Brogan's and Adrian Oktenberg's reading of Bishop as 'conscious resister,' Harrison's reading of a 'double point of view,' and Barbara Page's reading of her 'unofficial and unstable positionings'" (226).[1] In addition, Lynn Keller and Cristanne Miller's 1984 essay "Emily Dickinson, Elizabeth Bishop, and the Rewards of Indirection" set the stage for interpreting Bishop's related rhetorical strategies of complication and subterfuge such as camouflage and indirection. Dickie's *Stein, Bishop, Rich* has drawn attention to universalized heterosexual texts and lesbian subtexts in Bishop's work (85). Finally, Bishop's interrogation of the duplicity of language has received much attention from readers like Keller and Mutlu Blasing (*Remaking It New* 12; *Politics & Form* 88).

I am indebted to the thinking of Michel de Certeau's defining work on political resistance in chapter six of *The Practice of Everyday Life* for my framework for reading Bishop's four major negotiation strategies: visible complicity, quasi-visible dissent, quasi-(in)visible dissent, and confounding silence. Not surprisingly, his articulation of strategies of dissent fits in with dominant Bishop scholarship on her rhetorical prowess.

He states that a writer can struggle openly with politics in a climate of free discussion. He goes on to argue, however, that the writer must search for other subversive strategies of dissent during "moments" of suppression that are difficult to observe but not completely hidden [quasi-(in)visible]. These strategies include: 1) rewriting or parodying earlier poems, songs, and newspaper clippings or reporting on specific historical and cultural events, thereby creating "readerly" poems; 2) writing but not publishing in order to preserve the "moment" of suppression for a later, more open "moment" and audience; 3) multiple codings of published texts; 4) strategic self-censorship; and 5) silence.

In addition to contributing to Elizabeth Bishop studies, this book contributes to the history of twentieth-century American poetry; American cultural studies, especially the field of World War II–Cold War politics and culture; childhood studies; and gender and women's studies. No major studies of twentieth-century American poetry address the early development of the Cold War narrative along with the Second World War. Robert von Hallberg's pathbreaking *American Poetry and Culture, 1945–1980,* for instance, does not treat World War II, nor does Michael Davidson's recent germinal essay "Postwar Poetry & the Politics of Containment." The important work on the poetry of the Second World War by such seminal scholars as Schweik in *A Gulf So Deeply Cut* focuses solely on this war.

As this narrative on Bishop demonstrates, however, scholars in midcentury poetry need to consider the complex relationship that exists between the midcentury's victory story and the era's poets and poetry. The Cold War narrative is built so directly upon the World War II victory script that ignoring its origins is to miss a great deal of important poetic dialogue with it. Too little connection has been made between the role of poetry (and high culture) and the rethinking of midcentury cultural narratives. It has been widely assumed that the most important post–1945 poetry about peace and antimilitarism in this century was written during the Vietnam War Era by such poets as Denise Levertov, Audre Lorde, and Robert Lowell. This assumption continues in spite of evidence to the contrary. In addition, the Cold War cultural politics discussed in this book indicates that it strategically separated "high culture," including poetry, from politics and mass and popular culture. Our view of the apolitical and ahistorical nature of poetry is, then, partly a Cold War contrivance that can be revised.

When I attended the 1996 American Poetry in the 1950s Conference sponsored by the National Poetry Foundation, I discovered that Bishop was not only a major figure in twentieth-century American poetry but also a "forceful and continuing presence" in the canon of the 1950s (Roman, "Bishop at Orono, Maine: 'American Poetry in the 1950s' Conference," 2). But this presence did not come from a plenary session speech, a sure sign of canonization at a conference. It resulted from the presentation of nine papers in three sessions devoted exclusively to Bishop. Even more important, she also "'travelled' into papers in panel sessions on other poets and topics, into question-and-answer periods, into post-panel discussions in hallways, into conversations over meals, into plenary papers, and into post-plenary give-and-take" (2). She could be found everywhere but in the center itself of canonmaking: a plenary paper focused solely on her. This narrative will resituate Bishop more centrally within this canon, acknowledging how her "outsiderhood," as I learned from her subtle dominance from the margins of the conference, is also a position of power.

The first book-length treatment of a U.S. poet interested primarily in the dialogue between the poet's life and work and the national victory narrative, this book participates as well in ongoing conversations within the field of American cultural studies. Because recovering Bishop's complex multinarrative requires reading her in the political context of the war years and in relation to other forms of cultural production, including journalism and advertising, this project is more accurately a cultural narrative of Bishop. A single case study, it permits a consideration of Bishop's complex positioning as a dialogical process. Such a strategy works against the critical problem of reducing either her view or the multifaceted nature of agency and constraint, a tendency of group studies that are more interested in identifying and examining broad trends rather than in-depth "moments." This single study also enables one to pay close attention to the intertextuality between published writing and unpublished archival work. Moreover, it permits a close scrutiny of the problems and strategies of one "high culture" writer during the two major historical "moments" of the Second World War and the early Cold War and Korean War that may help to reinterpret other "high" cultural producers at this time.

This book, then, supplements two of the major pathbreaking book-length studies on cultural production during the midcentury narrative— Alan Nadel's *Containment Culture* and Engelhardt's *The Fall of Victory Culture*—that tend to privilege popular culture over high culture. While Nadel reads *The Catcher in the Rye,* for example, his work focuses primarily on film and other popular culture forms. Likewise, Engelhardt bolsters his arguments that the victory culture plot failed when the national government attempted to "package" the Vietnam conflict as another Hitler-like threat with examples from mass and commercial cultural production to show the gradual erosion in the public's trust in this narrative.

Because Bishop's story illustrates the long-term effects of civilian war trauma on children, it also contributes to the study of childhood and war.[2] Bishop's complex response to the midcentury victory culture narrative is related to her childhood, as well as ongoing, war trauma. Bishop lived most of her life with war. She associated her move to the United States from Canada with World War I. In her later Cold War–era memoir "The Country Mouse," she vividly recalled her resistance to learning "The Star-Spangled Banner" because she did not want to betray Canada (*The Collected Prose* 26). In addition, the large explosion during the First World War in Halifax Harbor after her move to the United States impressed her with the dangers of war for civilians since her mother was one of its victims.

When the navy began to set up its military base in Key West at the beginning of World War II, these earlier war traumas resurfaced in her correspondence to friends like Marianne Moore. She assumed evacuation was imminent once the navy had arrived and transformed the harbor. Then in 1950, when the Korean War started and Cold War containment was underway, Bishop began to plot out departure again. A fellowship awarded by

Bryn Mawr College enabled her to travel to Brazil and to establish her home there until the mid–1960s.

Finally, but not least, this study of Bishop also participates in conversations in gender and women's studies—most directly in the field described as the "mythology of gender and war" by gender and war historians Margaret and Patrice Higonnet. They argue that we need to rethink women's roles as agents and not simply as passive, Penelope-like victims in war, which "exculpates and extricates women from history" (2, 46). Special attention needs to be paid to the complexity of women's roles in a culture like "containment" that was war-driven but denied it. "Cold war" is as much "war" as "hot, declared war." Moreover, women's lives were deeply changed because of the war's military goals for the nation.[3] "Containment" actively attempted to force women to return to the home after World War II so that the returning military would have a public place in work and society. It differentiated between heterosexual, reproductive women and nonreproductive women, including lesbians like Bishop, rewarding the former and ostracizing the latter.

While the wounds of childhood war trauma and other competing needs help to account in part for Bishop's reclusiveness and desire for the sidelines, Bishop's understated but keen sense of marketplace politics also enabled her survival as a woman and lesbian during a troubled and turbulent time. She strategically withdrew into the culturally sanctioned role of the private woman hidden from public view. Then, with her protective circle of intimates, friends, and literary peers, she continued to promote this image of herself.

Because of her years living in Key West during the 1930s and 1940s and then in Brazil during the 1950s and 1960s, she seemed physically absent from the U.S. literary world. In her absence a dominant "Greta Garbo" image of reclusiveness and privacy emerged. (Coincidentally, Garbo was rumored to be a lesbian and hid from public view except in her films.)[4] This image belied such achievements as Bishop's national poetry appointment in 1949-50.

Both her actual absence and this Garbo-like hegemonic image made it appear unlikely that she concerned herself with U.S. politics and history in her work when the contrary is true. She seemed very convincing in her pursuit of what her friend, poet James Merrill, has described as "her lifelong impersonations of an ordinary woman," publishing highly-regarded poetry while following the acceptable role for "ordinary women" of shunning the public limelight and forum (259). Indeed, her image as a conventional woman and poet seemed to work to her advantage when it came to filling the poetry consultancy at a time when such poets as Langston Hughes and William Carlos Williams faced allegations of Communist sympathies and were found politically unacceptable for the job.[5] Yet Bishop found this "impersonation of an ordinary woman"—this performative identity, to use the cultural terms of Judith Butler in *Gender Trouble*— difficult to maintain at the Library of Congress. At the front of her journal of 1950 she announced that it was her "worst" year so far (Folder 77.4, Vassar College).

Because Bishop was positioned as an eyewitness looking out through a series of windows at the arriving World War II—Cold War victory narrative and culture, each chapter of this book is organized around a major unfolding scene. Chapter two resituates Bishop's personal narrative about her poetry career and private life in relationship to the nation's story through my interpretative window, or lens, for viewing her. It demonstrates the complexity of reading her unexamined cultural positions by considering her in relationship to popular culture's model midcentury hero John Wayne and by arguing for the merits of reading poetry, a high culture form, as an intertext with mass and popular culture forms. Finally, chapter two introduces my eclectic reading frame drawn from cultural studies, biography, historical scholarship, literary criticism, and archival research.

Chapters three and four consider Bishop's views of the arriving Second World War in Key West. Chapter three establishes the World War II interventionist narrative that evolved into the national victory narrative, which influenced gender and sexual roles as well as cultural production. I position Bishop's complex personal narrative about her poetry and private life in relation to Edna Millay's patriotic work. Chapter four interprets "Roosters" and the overlooked relevance of "Songs for a Colored Singer" as Bishop's other major Second World War statement. It reads "Roosters" as not only Bishop's widely acknowledged pre-Pearl Harbor intertwining of general militarist anxieties, but also as an expression of her concerns about civilian life in a military culture that involves questions of national identity, citizenship, culture, war, sexuality, gender, class, ethnicity, and race. In exploring "Songs for a Colored Singer," chapter four considers an unacknowledged statement on the war-era's racial violence and a complex quasi-(in)visible lesbian text.

Chapters five and six address Bishop's confounding views on V-Day 1945 and the poetry consultancy. Chapter five traces her struggles with the emerging Cold War culture, defining her constraints within the victory narrative ideology, more restrictive gender and sexual roles, and the surveillance of cultural production. It positions her skepticism in the unread archival poetry fragment, "V-Day August 14th, 1945," as a remarkable insight into the militarized and industrialized slaughters of the Second World War—the Holocaust in Europe, the Japanese annexations in Manchuria and China, the more global invasions of the Axis powers, and the Allied bombing of Germany and Japan. After contextualizing the women's media's attempted positioning of women poets through an interpretation of the World War II model patriot Millay in her unexamined depiction as "Poet's Kitchen" in a 1949 issue of *The Ladies' Home Journal,* it reads Bishop's depiction in a Boston newspaper's Sunday magazine story during her tenure at Library of Congress. The chapter ends by tracing major crises in her personal narrative about her poetry career and her private life, including Lowell's Communist accusations at Yaddo and the awarding of the Bollingen Prize for poetry to Ezra Pound.

Chapter six takes up Bishop's eyewitness report of Washington from her Library of Congress office, exploring her vacillation between speech and silence in the uninterpreted private writing in her journal of 1950, related correspondence, and poetry in order to trace her intertwined narratives of consent and dissent with Cold War culture and the Korean War. It examines her archival journal of 1950 in relation to both the largely ignored poem "View of the Capitol from the Library of Congress" and the canonical "Visits to St. Elizabeths" and "From Trollope's Journal."

Finally, chapter seven recovers more fully the relevance of the 1950 poem "Desk at Night," which she revised and expanded into "12 O'Clock News," revealing the crucial importance of this book's retrieval of Bishop's missing dialogue with the World War II–Cold War victory narrative.

Chapter 2 ➛

RE-VIEWING BISHOP:
FROM THE CRITIC'S DESK

Writing at a desk that looks through a window into a garden, I think about Bishop sitting in Washington—with the Cold War–embroiled U.S. Capitol in front of her instead of azaleas. But which Bishop(s) do I see, of the many public and private "versions" of Bishop suggested by the successful poet in the photo as well as the unhappy woman writing "worst year" so far in the private journal? In order to identify and understand these various "versions" of Bishop, we must resituate her in World War II–Cold War victory culture.

It is difficult to imagine a more oppositional coupling than Bishop and the jingoistic John Wayne in midcentury victory culture. While one might reposition Bishop in this historical "moment" in several ways, a cultural reading of Bishop's pairing with Wayne in the August 19, 1996, issue of *The New Yorker* will permit us to begin considering the public and private Bishop(s) of this book. Bishop and Wayne embraced polar opposite ends of the ideological spectrum, their respective public positionings clearly established in 1949.

According to the government record, Bishop was a nearly disabled, reclusive government employee who avoided the spotlight as much as possible in the poetry chair at the Library of Congress. Millier points out that she literally was away from her office desk much of the time, due to asthma attacks, alcoholic illness, and other autoimmune disorder problems ("The Prodigal," 60).

Wayne, in contrast, assumed the highly visible role of the model Cold War citizen as president of the Motion Picture Alliance for the Preservation of American Ideals, which monitored the movie industry for Communist activity and made movies celebrating the Second World War and the history of the nation's victory culture.[1] One of his most telling roles was the title role in the film *Big Jim McLain* often seen now on classic movie channels.[2] Here he depicts an FBI agent assigned to investigate suspected Communists in Hawaii after attending a hearing of the House Committee on Un-American Activities (HUAC).

The New Yorker's pairing of Bishop and Wayne featured "Easel by Elizabeth Bishop," which included two previously unpublished poems by Bishop for her Brazilian companion Lota de Macedo Soares and a watercolor of her Key West and New York lover Louise Crane, side by side with the middle section of the three-part essay "John Wayne's Body" by Garry Wills.[3] Wills's piece chronicles how the nation's popular culture has conflated its heroic Cold War image with Wayne's screen personae in such World War II–based films as *The Sands of Iwo Jima.*

Wayne's story—as Wills constructs it—is very much a matter of public, accessible, or highly visible record, offering an ideal fit with the national victory narrative that ensured its full assimilation as well as prominence. Indeed, the two seem interchangeable. During his greatest popularity at the height of Cold War containment "consensus," in which the majority of U.S. citizens viewed the Cold War effort as the most important goal of the United States, Wayne portrayed on the film screen the victory narrative's white male role of the heroic soldier. He played either the ideal American soldier saving the white nation of women and children during World War II or a Western cowboy "taming" the frontier and creating a nation from it.

He also pursued this "savior" war role offscreen as a private citizen, in a manner reminiscent of the private military-ready citizens of the Roman Empire. Wills reminds us in his essay that "America . . . had the sense of an *imperial* burden, which came to it with the Second World War and the Cold War. . . . America . . . made the President a full-time Commander-in-Chief even of non-military citizens" (47). Wayne "internalized its demands" (39). He served in 1949, as mentioned earlier, as a watchdog in Hollywood.

Wayne seemed the ideal patriot both in his life and his art, Wills recounts, because he had made war propaganda films during the Second World War and was selected by the World War II hero General Douglas MacArthur as the "ideal of an American soldier" (39). Wayne's own World War II victory narrative script was recycled into the Cold War version and became essential to it. Ironically, Wayne's propaganda role did not actually match reality because he did not serve in the war—yet his personality seemed to fit the desired "ideal soldier" more than, for instance, the quiet and private actor James Stewart, who served as a colonel and B–17 bomber commander in the Eighth Air Force.

Wayne's close personal and professional collaboration with the Cold War national victory culture led to his "performing body" becoming what I term a cultural synecdoche for this national narrative. Wills states: "The way to be an American was to be Wayne" (39). His white heterosexual male body became a text inscribed with the national myth of a victorious militarist salvific nation that could conquer "heathen" Communism. Wayne stood at the top of a hierarchy of male brotherhood within the Western history of war, militarism, and nationalism and proved to be a soldier worthy of the hearty welcome-home by women and children of the nation in this victory culture.

His willingness to fuse his body or personal narrative with the national body politic or national narrative led to his effectiveness in foreign and domestic politics and propaganda because he represented the ideal of one's proper love for the country or nation. In addition, he offered proof of the power of the Cold War U.S. nation to instill a desire to embrace the nation and thus to satisfy the need for love and allegiance, a desire for an eroticized nationalism that remains omnipresent globally (Parker, et. al., *Nationalisms & Sexualities* 1). Wayne was a male militant hero with whom other men could bond, regardless of nationality. Wills writes, "When . . . Henry Kissinger attributed his diplomatic success to Americans' admiration for cowboys who come into town alone, he was drawing on the Wayne legacy" (40). His portrayal of a powerful, salvific white heterosexual male on film empowered the national narrative's attempts to dominate the lives of its citizens. Wills says that "for decades, John Wayne haunted the dreams of Americans" (40).

In contrast to Wayne's fused public and private story in *The New Yorker*, Bishop's story in the World War II–Cold War victory culture narrative is more problematical to identify and to understand. The nation expected white women in the midcentury victory narrative to follow the traditional role for women in Western war that historians of gender, cultural production, and war have characterized as the role of Penelope (named for the classical heroine and wife of Ulysses) supporting and welcoming the military.[4] In addition to this "home front" role, the nation also directed white women to function in an age-old scenario whereby they requested and/or needed protection and/or rescue. This scene of threatened harm to white "Penelopes" and their children has long been the "battle cry" justifying the nation's defining narrative—the American war story of victory, according to Engelhardt (16-17).

Initially the collage of Bishop's World War II–Cold War era writing and art seems to reinforce the Penelope-like role of white women in victory culture that novelist Joan Didion depicts in the Wills essay on Wayne. Didion told Wills that Wayne's face had been so dominant in her dreams for so long that it was more familiar to her than her husband's: Wayne had become part of her most intimate private life (40). So Didion's private/public selves had merged with Wayne, as is expected of women in the Penelope role.

Bishop's depicted women also are shown in intimate moments in the bedroom. In the World War II–era watercolor "Sleeping Figure," the kimono-clad lover (Crane) seems to be asleep on a bed with an open book by her side. The poems "Foreign-Domestic" and "A Lovely Finish . . ." portray Soares reclining with a mystery book or waking up with her partner in the morning.

Wills's text on Wayne flanks Bishop's literary and private world on both sides of the two-page magazine layout or spread, imposing through textual proximity Wayne's relevance to her figures of women in the bedroom. On one hand, one can read Wayne as a victory culture soldier-savior guarding, with the two flanks of text, the women as apparently compliant Penelopes. Nothing in the Bishop collage visibly contradicts such a reading.

Yet nothing indicates a request and/or need for protection or rescue, or even "desire." This female-centered world (as well as lesbian-centered world for those who know Bishop's biography or life-text) seems self-contained and self-sufficient. Wayne thus can be read as both victory culture's imposing, unwelcome intruder into heterosexual Penelope's intimate world—and as a threat in lesbian life, seeking trial and imprisonment to ensure invisibility or erasure, in the words of lesbian theorist Terry Castle (7).[5]

While both readings indicate Bishop's dissent, they differ in one major respect. I would argue that Bishop's heterosexual, female-centered stance is amenable to victory culture's gendering and therefore quasi-visible, signaling acceptable dissent. The lesbian stance, however, is unacceptable and therefore quasi-(in)visible, signaling a high-risk position. So within dissent, fine lines of gradation distinguish between positions of risk.

But we need not stop here with these readings grounded in a female-centered gender and sexuality. The world of Penelope also refers to the larger white home front. The U.S. nation, like many European and European-derived nations, has conceived of itself in terms of white males equal soldiers-protectors-rescuers and white females equal threatened nation. In this binary division of male military and female home front, the nation codes women, nonmilitary men, and children as female. So Bishop's collage also offers three intertwined readings of militarism in midcentury victory culture: as guardian of the home front, unwelcome intruder, and threat to survival.

All these readings of the Bishop collage as commentary on the Penelope/civilian home front figure are valid. They differ in their accessibility to the reader. The readings of Bishop's visible apparent compliance and the quasi-visible dissent are derived solely from the juxtapositions of Bishop's women and poetry and Wayne in the magazine and thus are the most publicly accessible readings. The retrieval of Bishop's acceptable dissent, however, requires that readers work against the cultural norms of victory culture and agree that private citizens' anxieties about the national victory culture narrative constitute a valid subject for cultural interpretation.

In contrast to this quasi-visible dissent, the lesbian-focused reading of Bishop's quasi-(in)visible conflict with "Penelope" demands that readers be more informed about Bishop's biography to decode it and to consider the punitive attitude toward this subject-positioning. (Indeed, the published feature on Bishop subtly draws attention to her companion Lota but stops short of explicitly stating that they were lovers and hints not at all that the collage depicts two of Bishop's lovers.) Moreover, this interpretation requires that readers be willing to break with culturally normative heterosexist reading practices that automatically code a text as heterosexual.[6]

Equally important, this repositioning of Bishop as a poet of multiple codings requires that one not take so-called public silence at face value but rather search for what may lie behind the silence, where alternative writings might be located. This means approaching Bishop's archival work as at least equal with her published writing—as "fugitive" writing, to use Lombardi's word (5). This collage is a case in point. Before *The New Yorker's* editor Alice Quinn found these two poems in draft versions in the Bishop archives at Vassar College and then positioned them with the artwork located by William Benton for his book collection of Bishop's art, *Exchanging Hats,* this entire collage was unavailable. Only the poems' existence in the archives and the watercolor's presence in the art collection of Bishop executor Alice Mefthessel made this reading and the collage possible.[7]

The magazine collage illustrates that Bishop weaves the complicitous and oppositional together so finely that one cannot tell them apart easily. Some readers might argue that this destabilization of meaning itself proves that her main goal was subversion. Certainly a strategy of destabilization is crucial. But then one must also consider the nonpublication of the poems, the resulting apparent silence, the implied (self- or other) censorship, and her preservation of unpublished writing in her archives. In any case, a definition of political resistance based primarily on the published open and explicit protest poetry of the Vietnam era is inadequate for reading Bishop's work at this time. Her cultural production requires an interpretative lens that will account more centrally and fully for a wide range of subtle strategies and that will avoid any tendency to reduce her decisions to simple binaries: for/against war, complicity/subversiveness, silence/protest, and so forth.

As discussed in the introduction, de Certeau's defining work on political resistance informs my framework for reading Bishop's four major negotiation strategies of visible complicity, quasi-visible dissent, quasi-(in)visible dissent, and confounding silence. Bishop's strategies in her writing during World War II and Cold War "containment" anticipate de Certeau's analysis of resistance. Bishop's archives, for instance, provide an invaluable coequal corpus of her work for addressing fractious questions about her political and cultural positionings, helping one to sort out the ramifications behind Bishop's silences, strategic self-censorship, multiple codings of published texts, and unpublished work. This state of textual affairs is hardly accidental, especially for a poet facing severe cultural constraints. It forces a reevaluation of the privileged position accorded both published writing as a whole and the published version of a given poem. Treating the archival writing equally with the published writing results in an informative "intertext." Archival writing, with its problematical issues of incompletion, fragmentation, and textual and intertextual disarray, can tease out what the published work conceals under the illusion of closure. The "intertext" can reveal not only which part of a writer's work was amenable to national politics and the literary/cultural marketplace reifying and reproducing it, but also what the writer decided to omit.

We cannot afford to ignore the fact that Bishop deposited her papers in the archives, thereby leaving them as another vital part of her literary and cultural work for reconsideration. Bishop went to great lengths to preserve her manuscript legacy, Travisano has correctly pointed out, "spending weeks on the packing and shipping of her materials from Brazil after Lota's death, at a time when it was no longer pleasant or comfortable to live there" ("The Elizabeth Bishop Phenomenon," 233).

While de Certeau's delineation of political strategies illuminates the complexity of Bishop's negotiations, closer but brief examination here of both "Roosters" and "12 O'Clock News" also offers crucial insight into her thinking process that moves beyond even de Certeau's comprehensive framework. These poems reveal that at times even her public antimilitarist statements in the open periods of dissent about each war may camouflage high-risk, quasi-(in)visible disagreement. During World War II, it is true that Bishop publicly denounced militarism in "Roosters." But it is also crucial to remember that she did so before the bombing of Pearl Harbor, with the indirect poetic devices of allegory and biblical story, at a time when many poets of various political factions were writing antiwar poems. Moreover, readers since Moore have read the poem primarily as a denunciation of European Fascism, a political interventionist positioning strongly encouraged at the time by President Franklin Roosevelt in the national debate about whether the United States should enter the war. So for many readers Bishop's antimilitarism actually placed her politics in the same camp with those of the president and other poets like Edna St. Vincent Millay.

Not until Bishop wrote her famous letter to Moore on "Roosters," which will be discussed later, was it also possible to conjecture that she had included her anxieties about militarism in the United States in her view about the "baseness" of militarism. Thus she had interwoven both the growing hegemonic view and her concerns together so finely that one could not easily discern between them.

The same confounding strategies characterize the widely acclaimed "12 O'Clock News" published in the mid–1970s well after public outcry against the Vietnam War. Even though this was a period of open war dissent, Bishop never explicitly refers to the Vietnam War or to Vietnam itself in the poem. Indeed, one of the most apocalyptic messages in the poem is its sense that the war is global as well as specific to one war front.

Both published poems signal Bishop's complex and provocative politics as well as her cautiousness. Based on her subtle rhetorical maneuvering during an *open period* of national cultural debate, it is not unexpected to find a dense *reader-resistant* textuality in the *less open* decade following "Roosters" as Bishop's anxieties about self-protectiveness increased. Regarding the Second World War period, Travisano has observed correctly that "the case can be made that the war daunted her creatively: she published nothing at all in either 1942 or 1943 and her production during the war was limited by even her own standards" (*Elizabeth Bishop* 73).

Two major views help to account for Bishop's silence at this time by suggesting that it was a strategy for handling marketplace and antimilitarist politics. Dickie argues that Bishop may have wanted to avoid tension with such poetry mentors and allies as Lowell and Moore who were writing poetry on war (106). Certainly she kept her eye on marketplace politics and wanted to avoid alienating her mentor Moore. There is no record, however, of her important friendship with Lowell at this time, nor is there any comment about him. Goldensohn states that Bishop may not have wanted to compromise her general antimilitarist positioning and preferred public silence instead, an important insight into Bishop's conscience and actions (*Elizabeth Bishop* 157). Yet Bishop's attempt at defense work in Key West also indicates another, more accepting view of the war in addition to her antimilitarism.

The reconsidered Bishop of this book is more congruent with the earlier contradictory "versions" of Bishop in the 1930s, with her appearances in the anti-Stalinist but American leftist *Partisan Review* while she enjoyed a privileged, comfortable, protected, and waited-on life in such places as Key West. [8] The poems "Unbeliever" and "Quai," for instance, appeared in the August–September 1938 issue alongside Leon Trotsky's "Art and Politics" and Victor Serge's "Marxism in Our Time." "The Fish" followed Stephen Spender's war chronicle "September Journal" in the March–April 1940 issue (Harrison 77). I am not suggesting that she was using her poetry consciously to create a politicized "voice" in an international dialogue, but that she found it politically comfortable to publish in the journal.

Since Bishop's anxieties about the impact of a military state in "Roosters" are intertwined cautiously with her anti-Fascism, one might conjecture that she would express her views after the landmark events of the bombing of Pearl Harbor or the U.S. air bombing of Japan in a highly secretive manner. For instance, silence, when one expects a publicly articulated position, is one way to register such resistance. Multiple codings of poems offer another strategy. The poem "Songs for a Colored Singer" for Billie Holiday published in 1944 and the unpublished archival fragment entitled "V-Day August 14th, 1945" reveal that Bishop did exactly this. She continued to think about the war and its accompanying victory culture using the dissent strategies of song parody, multiple codings of published texts, written but unpublished texts, self-censorship, and silence. In "Songs for a Colored Singer," Bishop encodes quasi-visible concerns. She also addresses racism through quasi-visible dissent and homophobia through quasi-(in)visible dissent.

Her poetry fragment for V-Day challenges Bishop's assumed silence at this historical "moment." Questioning the victory parade that celebrated the end of World War II, she could not finish her thoughts. She left them, however, in her archival papers for later generations of readers to find and read for not only what she wrote, but also for a visual handwritten record of how her halting language falls into silence: how her cultural representation breaks into fragments.

On Bishop's so-called silence while she was poetry consultant to the Library of Congress during the outbreak of the Korean War, Millier and Dickie have concluded that, in Dickie's words, this experience "provided few subjects for poems," other than "View of the Capitol from the Library of Congress" and the later "Visits to St. Elizabeths" and "From Trollope's Journal," and that she suffered from illness (Dickie 112; Millier, *Elizabeth Bishop* 219-22). However, such apparent blatant silence also seems too incongruent to ignore.

Bishop's anxieties about militarization in the United States from World War II placed her in conflict with Cold War Washington and national expectations for poets. When MacLeish served as Librarian at the Library of Congress during the war, he had spearheaded patriotic poetry and directed the war of information. Anyone in a position such as the poetry consultancy faced the prospect of being called upon in the Cold War or Korean War. Although many must have expected Bishop to assume a more patriotic role eventually, she did not do it.

She also did not attempt to revive the patriotic woman poet's role from this war usually associated with Millay. In part this may be due to the more public role that Bishop's mentor and friend Moore had begun to assume with her war poetry—i.e., "In Distrust of Merits." A member of Millay's generation, Moore seems to have filled this patriotic woman poet's role in the 1950s. In 1951 and 1952 she won the Pulitzer Prize, the National Book Award, and the Bollingen Prize; and as Bishop writes in her much later memoir-tribute, "Efforts of Affection," Moore then became famous as a baseball fan and faithful admirer of Presidents Herbert Hoover and Dwight Eisenhower (*The Collected Prose* 154). But one must not overlook the fact that Bishop was in a position to compete for this role if she had wanted it. Indeed, she took the Library of Congress job after Moore had refused it.

Bishop's politics alone would have presented high-risk conflict in this victory culture, adding to her tensions as an apparent consummate Cold War national culture "insider" at the Library of Congress with her culturally sanctioned positioning as a white, financially secure, Vassar-educated, New England woman poet. This confounded subjectivity would have made it imperative for her to function as what Paul Smith has called the "discerning subject": "not simply the *actor* who follows ideological scripts, but . . . also as an *agent* who reads them in order to insert him/herself into them—or not" (6). But her lesbian identity further intensified her contradictory high-risk position in a Cold War homophobic culture with its label of "outsider" (Rich, "The Eye of the Outsider" 127, 131). So when Bishop read the midcentury victory script to decide whether or not to insert herself and how, she had to weigh her options based upon the need to consider wide-ranging concerns, including militarization and her sexual affiliation.

Complicating her confounded cultural positioning even further were the political upheavals in the poetry world of the early Cold War. She faced the disarray of the elite art colony Yaddo, where she lived in 1949 and again in 1950 just after Lowell, Flannery O'Connor, Elizabeth Hardwick, and others had accused the director, Elizabeth Ames, of Communist involvement. In addition, she found herself in a poetry consultancy that had been recently ravaged by the furor over the incarcerated Pound's receipt of the Bollingen Prize administered by the Library of Congress and its subsequent removal to Yale University's administrative oversight.

To manage these political conflicts, this narrative argues that Bishop continued to turn to strategies of assent, visible compliance, quasi-visible dissent, quasi-(in)visible dissent, and silence during her one-year government poetry consultancy at the Library of Congress. The deconstruction of the Cold War national capital and its victory narrative became the subject of work either written at this time or later, but directly based upon this year. Bishop thus made strong use of the tactic of delayed writing and publication until a more politically accommodating "moment" as well as other dissenting tactics.

She later rewrote, for instance, the nursery rhyme "This is the House that Jack Built" to portray the antiheroic Ezra Pound whom she visited as part of her poetry consultancy while he lived in hospital confinement for his treason during World War II. She also cautions against the antiheroic role of the poet in any military state narrative and thus points the reader in an autobiographical direction, for she was sitting in the national government post for U.S. poets at the time.

She appropriated Anthony Trollope's journal observations about Civil War–era Washington D.C. to launch a concealed attack on Eisenhower and the so-called heroic history of the Cold War national narrative in "From Trollope's Journal." But this poem also holds unrecognized autobiographical importance as a disguised gesture toward her unpublished archival commentary of her own year in Washington in her journal of 1950.

Finally, she reported on an Air Force band concert in "View of the Capitol from the Library of Congress," coding the published poem to question Cold War—and Korean War—tactics and leaving in the archives a more provocative agenda in earlier versions and fragments than the published poem leads the reader to expect.

In 1950 she began as well to circulate to her former lover Margaret

Miller and *The New Yorker* editor Katherine White an early full draft of a poem entitled "Desk at Night," which contains another crucial part of her basic critique of Cold War victory narrative. This poem offers an extraordinary example of writing during a "moment" of suppression and waiting for a more open political climate. She did not publish it then because it was not accepted (*One Art* 114). But she did not abandon it. Instead she developed it over a period of more than twenty years into the Vietnam-era published poem "12 O'Clock News."

Finally, she left the 1950 journal in the archives that helps to reveal, along with this other work, that her year in Washington was a watershed time of thinking about war and militarism. In this unpublished journal, she set down notes about her visits to Pound, her drafts of "View of the Capitol from the Library of Congress," and reflections on her personal life in the Cold War–torn landscape of Washington. The journal offers a matrix of raw material for all three published poems; so it is the crucial text for the year, revealing the extent to which her Cold War positioning was confounded.

Bishop's politics place her on "cutting-edge" conversations about gender, race, class, culture, war, and nationalism. Like Engelhardt and Nadel, she read the nuclear-driven militarized Cold War national narrative as potentially dangerous and manipulative. Like Milton Bates in his *The Wars We Took to Vietnam,* she understood that the discourse of war is intertwined with the related, competing discourses of race, nationalism, class, generational difference, territorial expansion, and gender.

Moreover, she discerned that this midcentury narrative's identifiable literary form or convention as a heterosexual courtly romance (the Penelope and Ulysses story) and male rivalry/bonding ritual is related not only to earlier U.S. versions of the victory narrative but to European national narratives as well. She would have been sympathetic toward George Mosse's pioneering study *Nationalism & Sexuality* in which he argues that the late-eighteen-century European nation-building that influenced U.S. nation-building was tied to a heterosexual convention in which the white heterosexual female came to represent the nation in need of protection by the white heterosexual male.

Finally, Bishop realized that women hold symbolic or iconic relations to Euro-American national narratives as well as actor or agent relationships. She would have found the observations of Floya Anthias and Nira Yuval-Davis in *Women, Nation, State* vital. Here they state that women reproduce new citizens as well as inculcate the national ideology in new generations;

serve as symbols in the national discourse; help defend the nation through participation in its struggles; and, most usefully, act as "passive wards who require the state's protection," who may be asked to demand this protection as a patriotic gesture (7).

My construction of Bishop's agency in developing a dissenting position also depends upon locating a theory about the circulation of power inside a nation that can help explain how this dissidence can occur. Louis Althusser's work seems to directly address the social dynamics of a military-dominated narrative and nation. Challenging free agency in such a repressive state, he points out that both the official government system and the "ideological apparatus" of schools, mass media, the church, and other social institutions ensure "subjection to the ruling ideology" (133; 142-45; 176). Yet this view of the state and citizen interaction does not help to explain fully how a writer like Bishop could dissent, whether through preserving such writing in the archives for future generations or in multiply-coding published work with interrelated layers of consent and dissent.

The work of Michel Foucault, Pierre Bourdieu, and Antonio Gramsci offers a more insightful understanding of Bishop's position as a citizen-poet speaker. Foucault tells us that a social body's power and reality depend upon discourse; thus a national narrative legitimizes the power structure and actions of a social body like a nation:

> [T]here are manifold relations of power which permeate, characterize, and constitute the social body, and these relations of power cannot themselves be established, consolidated, nor implemented without the production, accumulation, circulation, and functioning of a discourse. (*Power/Knowledge* 93)

Bourdieu, like Foucault and unlike Althusser, sees power as diffuse, concealed, and often unquestioned, but hypothesizes that cultural production is integral to the reproduction of social structures and legitimizes dominant economic and political power (2). In describing the material organization maintaining the ideological structure of a dominant class, Gramsci depicts the essential roles of publishing houses, newspapers, periodicals, libraries, schools, associations, books, architecture, and so forth: in short, everything that can influence public opinion (389). Both Gramsci and Bourdieu help to establish why Bishop faced a very difficult struggle in positioning herself in midcentury victory culture.

Their theories also go a long way in interpreting how the cultural and literary marketplace that confronted Bishop became interlinked with the government system. With World War I, the national government ushered in a propaganda system that operated in the kind of way that both Bourdieu and Gramsci have theorized. This system ensured the engineering of national consent from many sectors of power, thus dispelling the charge that the federal government was functioning as a military state demanding the subjugation of citizens. This propaganda machinery functioned solely to articulate the victory culture narrative and to form the grounding of similar articulations of it in World War II and the Cold War. Its primary goal was to use all forms of cultural production to legitimize the nation's war story. James Mock and Cedric Larson, historians of the Committee on Public Information during World War I, later described the committee that became the model for later propaganda "think tanks" as a "gargantuan advertising agency the like of which the country had never known, and the breathtaking scope of its activities was not known until the rise of totalitarian dictatorships after the war" (27).

The success of the engineering of national consent for war rested primarily on the large-scale cultural reproductions of the national victory narrative. Not surprisingly, the all-male personnel as well as the androcentric focus of the World War I public information committee conform to nationalism theorists' views on the national narrative in nation-building. Benedict Anderson, for example, places the power of this kind of social discourse in the hands of "imagined communities" of men or a "passionate brotherhood" that create a kind of "storyline," to conceive of itself as a nation" (*Imagined Communities* 15-16). Once the storyline is developed, it is used to unify its citizens as a nation. Postcolonialist Homi Bhabha argues that the nation grows because of this narrative, which creates subject-citizens. A nation, he explains, is often found "in the disclosures of its every day life," where "the very act of narrative performance creates a growing circle of national subject-citizens" (see *Nation & Narration*).

A citizen's personal narrative like Bishop's is part of this "narrative performance" of national subject-citizens. The question is whether this personal narrative merely subjects itself to and reflects the national narrative or refracts and dialogues with it. Nadel points out that it can be both congruent with and differentiated from the national narrative (11). Bishop appears both to synchronize with but also to dissent from this national victory narrative. The result is a dialogical narratology with levels of interrelated consent and dissent, an interpretation informed by Gramsci's theory of cultural hegemony and counterhegemony ("contradictory consciousness" always accompanies the ideas of a ruling group that creates consensus) and Bhaba's position that "no privileged narrative of the nation" exists.[9]

National multinarratives, as scholars like Bhaba and Bates have suggested, coexist on many levels of power and discourse. Much scholarship supports the notion of national multinarratives. John Lewis Gaddis, for example, argues that each Cold War national administration reinterpreted the national narrative to write its own narrative (43). The narrative of Harry Truman differed considerably from the narrative of Dwight Eisenhower. Moreover, the Roosevelt World War II narrative adapted by Truman and George Kennan to write a version of the Cold War national narrative should not be confused with the Cold War narrative espoused by the more exploitative, right-wing politicians Joseph McCarthy, Richard Nixon, and J. Edgar Hoover.[10]

In addition to multinarratives within the federal government and dialogical personal and national narratives, intertwined narratives exist between the media and the national culture. Wendy Kozol, in her study of *Life* magazine during the Cold War era in *Life's America,* illustrates that the media participating in the national narrative offered conflicting dialogical narratives. For example, while *Life* promoted the consensus view of "containment," idealizing the life of the white, upwardly mobile suburban family as equally available and desirable for all races, classes, and sexualities, the gap between the text and the photos revealed a nation in conflict, with no dominant consensus. Kobena Mercer, in studies of race and nation narrative recodings, has found that cultural production (from the popular and mass culture venues of newspapers and radio to the high culture of theater, fiction, and poetry) can offer both the sanctioned national romance narrative as well as counter-narratives or co-narratives, thereby creating a multinarrative ("Recoding" 19–26).

Nadel theorizes in *Containment Culture* that within the larger narrative structure of the courtship romance, multiple stories also circulate expressing a variety of positions. Both national cultural narratives and personal narratives can coexist. Often the two interact or fuse; sometimes, the larger national narrative attempts to contain the personal (3–4). "Under the name 'containment,'" according to Nadel, "we have generated numerous, often contradictory or mutually exclusive stories, each grounding its authority in the claim that it is part of the same story" (18).

The concept of a Bakhtinian dialogical victory culture narrative built around the conventions of courtship and male rivalry or bonding opens up a potential space for varying levels of consent and dissent about nationalism and war. In reading Bishop's narrative, however, it becomes clear that some speakers and types of narratives are more preferred and assimilated than others. Not all speakers, for example, are heard equally, nor are all stories allowed full voice. The competent poet, the cautious lesbian, the "lover" of privilege, the frightened child—these versions of Bishop and the many others discussed in this book must compete.

By the time Bishop reached Cold War Washington, she had developed several strategies for negotiating her private and pubic selves from her experience with the Second World War. The next chapter examines the Roosevelt administration's interventionist war narrative that reached out to all sectors of the nation, including poets and writers. It will compare and contrast the public poetic stance of the "patriotic" woman poet Millay with Bishop's personal narrative during the war.

Chapter 3 ⟿

IN KEY WEST OVERLOOKING WORLD WAR II

In 1940 Bishop sat in her writing studio in a Key West, Florida, hotel that was built like a ship—with "all white paint, shutter doors, long red carpets, and views of the ocean"—and watched the U.S. Navy turn her private civilian world into a naval base. She wrote Marianne Moore on June 8:

> It is so pretty—but more and more Navy ships keep coming, and they are building a tremendous airplane hangar. I am very much afraid that this is the last season we'll be able to live here for a long time. (*One Art* 91)[1]

For the reader acquainted with the World War I literary conventions of war poets like Rupert Brooke and Wilfred Owen or the literary and cultural work of Paul Fussell's *The Great War & Modern Memory* and Allyson Booth's *Postcards from the Trenches,* Bishop's letter evokes an irony associated with the Great War: war's destruction of pastoral beauty and innocence. As Bishop explains to Moore, she could watch the U.S. Navy create a naval base out of her "pretty" private civilian world, emphasizing the feminization and domestication of the land with her use of the adjective "pretty."

Like a ghost behind this summer of 1940 in Key West sits another, pre–Great War summer, however: the summer of 1914 when the world of British Empire privilege cracked open after its final season of lolling outside on folding canvas chaises while reading, swimming, walking in the countryside, picnicking, having tea on white wicker tables under trees (Fussell, *The Great War and Modern Memory* 24). For Bishop, this pre–World War I season of innocence held a special meaning, for this also was the last time that she enjoyed her own world of childhood in Nova Scotia with her ill mother and her mother's family. During the war, her father's family arranged for her to be brought to the United States to live since her mother could not care for her.

Bishop's appropriation of Great War literary irony against the imminent "unwanted war" in the letter to Moore tips her view, on one hand, in a political direction. Bemoaning the arrival of the navy rather than welcoming it with enthusiasm as a sign of future victory over Hitler and the Axis, she regrets the advent of war and the interventionist narrative of the Franklin Roosevelt administration. On the other hand, she also sounds like an upper-class young woman of financial independence who is becoming painfully aware that her sheltered world of literature, culture, leisure, and privilege is about to change forever, just as her childhood world changed.

Bishop's concern that the navy's arrival means that she will need to move—that it will displace her—is always the grim reality of war for civilians and soldiers alike. Battlegrounds draw soldiers toward them as civilians flee. So Bishop was prescient about the war's impact upon her and the nation. Her sense of entitlement to a peaceful private world would not protect her literary or private life from the effects of war. Militarization of any kind, but especially Fascism and Communism, frightened her. A civilian woman in a major military center who nearly lost her house to navy construction, Bishop was placed in a unique position for viewing the collapse between the military and civilian worlds.

Bishop seems to have understood what we learned only later—that war installations were mixed in and sometimes hidden by the civilian world. Photographs document, for example, a camouflaged suburban scene in California that looked real to an enemy aircraft but was only an illusion sewn on camouflaged netting to cover the war-factory complex beneath it (Muschamp 51). Key West likely also used such devices.

Books about World War II fill bookshelves, so this chapter will not attempt to present a definitive history here in order to resituate Bishop within the larger historical "moment" storming around her. Instead it will provide an entry into the nation's war narrative—its crucial "happenings," the U.S. national government's discourse, the inflammatory debates about U.S. involvement, and the raging cultural politics. All of these pressed upon Bishop as she pursued her fledgling literary career and a private life of tumultuous romance.

We have been told repeatedly in our popular anecdotal mythology of the war that many observers in the United States and much of Europe had become fearful of another world war almost immediately after the Treaty of Versailles at the end of the Great War. So the notion of a peaceful private life, like the one to which Bishop seems to have felt entitled, was never secure for many between the wars. Astute observers had grown more alarmed with the rise of Hitler's government and military buildup during the 1930s. When the Japanese invaded Manchuria in 1931, Mussolini took over Ethiopia in 1935, and Hitler occupied the Rhineland in 1936, tensions escalated even further.

Then, when the Spanish Civil War began, many became convinced that total European war was imminent, especially with Hitler's and Mussolini's aid to Franco in 1937. Others worried about an Asian war when the Japanese attacked China in the same year. The pace of international war quickened as Hitler occupied Austria in 1938 and then took over Czechoslovakia. The Holocaust that consumed Jews, homosexuals, gypsies, dissidents, artists, teachers, intellectuals, Soviet prisoners of war, people with disabilities, and other peoples of conscience was underway. Refugees sought asylum outside of Hitler's reach in countries around the globe, including the United States.

While many in the United States concerned themselves with a narrative of anti-Fascism, still others feared the Soviet Union and the global spread of Communism and took part in a narrative of anti-Communism. Although some in this group eventually came to believe that the Soviet Union could help destroy Fascism, many held onto the belief that Fascism was the best way to control the growth of Communism and that this goal must be achieved at all costs.

The fear of Communism proved very damaging, as we now know, because it colluded with U.S. religious and racial bigotry, anti-Semitism, and xenophobia. It meant that the opportunity to save lives from Hitler's genocidal goals through the admission of refugees into the United States was lost because Roosevelt was focused on winning public and congressional support for the war and did not want to risk alienation over the refugee question (Goodwin 101-4, 174-76, 396-97). In addition, American Roman Catholics found the Vatican in Italy publicly silent on Fascism and therefore faced a gap in their church leadership about the war at a time when they might have become advocates of anti-Fascism. This resulted in both confusion about the U.S. role in the war and the loss of many lives in the Holocaust, outcomes that continue to be the subject of heated debate today.[2]

In fact, some in the very generation who would fight in the war did not even learn about the Soviet Union in the classroom and therefore were largely ignorant of Soviet affairs. Eleanor Roosevelt reported in 1933 that a fourth-grade history class had "a map of the world with a great big white spot on it—no name—no information. And the teacher told her that it was blank, with no name, because the school wouldn't let him say anything about that big blank space" (Goodwin 550-51).

Moreover, fears about Communism strongly influenced cultural politics. MacLeish, for instance, endured a very laborious and inflamed appointment process to his position as Librarian at the Library of Congress because of J. Parnell Thomas, Republican congressman from New Jersey and the chair of the House's Special Committee to Investigate Un-American Activities (Donaldson 295). MacLeish was labeled a "fellow traveler," a coded term for a socialist and/or Communist sympathizer (Graham 105). MacLeish later recalled:

> There were elements in public life in America who regarded support of the democratic government of Spain as equivalent to membership in the Communist party because the Russians had intervened in Spain, once Hitler and Mussolini had intervened on the side of Franco. So there was a good deal of yammering on the ground that I was probably also a Communist. (Donaldson 132)

Countless others questioned war for other reasons. They were pacifist or antimilitarist. Many felt that the First World War had revealed the utter futility and baseness of any kind of future war and approached a second world war as a mere repetition of the first. They felt shielded from the growing war by the Neutrality Acts of the mid–1930s.

Not surprisingly, Bishop was very preoccupied with war during the interwar period as public debate increased with the series of war events and atrocities. She found the war in Spain "frightening" (OA 45). A poem entitled "War in Ethiopia" that is now lost, according to Dickie, was offered to Horace Gregory in 1937 for a poetry collection (109; OA 55-56). She also offered to translate Spanish poems about the civil war for Rolfe Humphries in 1937 (OA 60). But her travel in Europe during the mid–1930s provided her with the opportunity to observe the growing climate herself and proved to be even more important than these literary gestures.

Millier says that during the early 1930s "she recorded a series of transparent dreams that link the tools of her trade, particularly typewriters, with images suggesting war. In one dream, the typewriter keys are a code she must solve" (134). Between these dreams and another war-haunted dream that Bishop transcribed in her notebook sometime during the late thirties after her European sojourn, we can discern that the travels prompted her imagination to consider war with the kind of depth and range that we associate with her major World War II masterwork, "Roosters" (Golden-sohn 156):

> many more dreams—almost every night. Tanks, lost in crowds of refugees, bombardments, etc. Last night I dreamed I heard cannon and that I was explaining to someone (we were standing beside a plaster-wall covered with bullet-marks) that it sounded exactly like the cooing of doves amplified 2 thousand times and "stretched out"—such & such a degree—and that there was some connection with that and the Peace Dove. (In the movies 2 days ago hardly noticed how the sound bullets make or at least the sound the movies make them make, really gives the effect of young birds starting to sing in spring.) (Box 75, Vassar College)[3]

A journal entry like this indicates the extent to which the language of war used in "Roosters" results from extended years of meditation and writing and not just one precipitating event. Indeed this prose passage offers two superlative examples of intertextual dialogue with "Roosters." The amplification of the "cooing of doves" that sounds like cannon in her diary is very similar to the poem's opening. The "first crow," followed by an "echo" and then an "insistence" that "flares" and "all over town begins to catch," is accompanied by an amplification of the sound of the roosters (*The Complete Poems* 35).[4] Then the "plaster-wall covered with bullet marks" in the journal passage seems as if it has been transposed into the "dropping-plastered henhouse floor" in the poem (35).

This intertextuality is not surprising, given the war-related context and imagery of much of Bishop's other poetry written about the same time and collected in her first volume *North & South* published in 1946. Poet Louise Bogan, one of the volume's earliest reviewers, pointed out in the October 5, 1946, issue of *The New Yorker* that it "contains all manner of references to war and warriors" (113). More recently, Schweik has reemphasized the theme of war in the collection: "Bishop's first book might be read, in fact, as a war book *in-directed*. In it the matters of war literature—naval engagements, border crossings, skirmishes, search missions, even a monument of sorts—appear, but only as covert operations" (213).

The collection opens with "The Map," one of the first poems that Bishop published, which reveals in its final lines that the apparent objective activity of mapmaking to represent geography may function in colonial conquest or "an activity . . . of military alignment" (Brogan, "Planets on the Table" 266). Bishop also links mapmaking to the creation of national identities, for the map may function as a text of national shared history that the conquerors wish to impose upon the conquered. As nationalism theorist Benedict Anderson explains, "imperial states" colored "their colonies on maps" (175).

Another of Bishop's earliest poems, in the volume, "Casabianca," "outrageously flouts," as Dickie states, "its predecessor's [Felicia Hemans's nineteenth-century poem on the Napoleonic wars] sentimental celebration of willful military sacrifice. Imaging love as 'the obstinate boy,' Bishop subverts filial devotion as well as military discipline" (110). From this poem, then, the reader learns that 'the boy on the burning deck,' who tried to recite as the ship went down in flames, is victimized by the militarist convention of male bonding and the heroic myths of war.

Moreover, in such poems as "Wading at Wellfleet" with its focus on "one of the Assyrian wars," which revise earlier war poems, Schweik suggests that Bishop focuses on "poetry's promotional and disciplinary functions in modern Western war systems" (236). So the reader also learns that militarism or victory culture may use poetry to victimize its targets, a point made by Anderson. He explains that nations inspire love, and often profoundly self-sacrificing love. The cultural products of nationalism—poetry, prose fiction, music, the plastic arts—show this love very clearly in thousands of different forms and styles. This love can be turned into "justification for invasion of the 'other'" (89).

Dickie has argued astutely that Bishop "seemed unable to avoid" war in the 1930s "even if she did not treat it directly often" (107). Other poems in her first collection, drawn from her travels in Europe, like "Sleeping on the Ceiling," "Place de la Concorde," "Sleeping Standing Up," "Paris, 7 a.m.," and "The Monument," all contain military and war imagery (107-10). So war was never far from Bishop's mind, either directly or marginally, during the interwar period.

The intensity of her concern about the coming war seemed to grow dramatically as war approached, with her poetry matching letters like the June 1940 missive to Moore. As Axelrod astutely contends, "The Fish," published in the March/April 1940 issue of the anti-Stalinist, leftist *Partisan Review* following Stephen Spender's war chronicle "September Journal" and written during the same period as "Roosters," offers a direct and profound reflection on the "battered and venerable" survivor, or military veteran, with his medals and ribbons ("The Middle Generation and WWII," 24-26).

But this does not mean that Bishop was prepared to embrace fully an interventionist position because of her anxieties about Fascism as did Eleanor Roosevelt, a pacifist from the privileged class in the World War I era who quickly assessed the dangers of Hitler and Mussolini and supported intervention completely by 1937. Bishop was suspicious of militarism and totalitarianism of any kind and only reluctantly realized that the war preparations in Key West were necessary. She was skeptical about Fascism and especially Communism. She became anti-Communist during the 1930s, positioning herself as a "socialist" and "left" with a great admiration for Auden, but "always anti-communist . . .—after one or two John Reed Club affairs," apparently repelled by the political dogmatism (Palattella 22). While many of her liberal friends hoped that Communism could defeat Fascism and supported its efforts, Bishop did not share their optimism.

She complained in a letter dated February 7, 1938, to her friend Frani Blough about a lunch she attended with Philip Rahv, Mary McCarthy, and Frederick Dupee, all connected with *Partisan Review,* in which they lambasted the Communists as Trotskyites the entire time. The experience left her ready to declare herself an anarchist (*OA* 68–69). Shortly after the lunch, Bishop bought a house in Key West with her friend and lover Crane and moved there (*OA* 68–69). The house at 624 White Street, still standing today and preserved in a painting by the primitivist Gregorio Valdes, featured two-story pillars in the front, an overhanging roof, and a porch beneath. Key West appealed to them with its open but poor society—a mix of WPA artists and intellectuals among the Americans, Cubans, Bahamians, Germans, and Irish, including Ernest Hemingway and John Dewey as residents and Wallace Stevens among the visitors.

Louise Crane, heiress to the Crane paper fortune, was a "life of the party" personality, and Bishop found herself at the center of Key West society. In fact, Crane was so lively that Bishop decided to take the little hotel room that she described in the letter to Moore so that she could write in the mornings away from the bustle of the house. Bishop filled her letters to friends on the mainland with social events, describing friends like John Dewey's daughter, the physicist Jane Dewey, and her friend and possible lover Tom Wanning, for whom she wrote "Little Exercise" (Millier 166; *CP* 41).

Given Bishop's concerns about international politics and the opportunity to observe preparations for a naval base beginning with Roosevelt's visit to Key West on February 19, 1939, the intensified navy buildup that she reported to Moore on June 8, 1940, probably did not surprise her. German interests in the Caribbean were well known; and Roosevelt himself had accompanied the U.S. Marines to Haiti to pacify the island and to write the new Haitian constitution allegedly in order to prevent Haiti from becoming a German naval base during World War I (Cook, *Eleanor Roo-*

sevelt, v. 1, 212-13). Moreover, later in 1939, the *St. Louis* with 930 Jewish passengers aboard had attempted to disembark at both Havana, Cuba, and Miami. After weeks of pleading with the Roosevelt administration to permit the refugees to obtain at least temporary sanctuary in Miami, the ship finally was forced to return to Europe, where most of its passengers perished (Goodwin 102).

Roosevelt's war concerns intensified on May 10, 1940, when the tensions within the European continent erupted into the open. The German aggression ended a period of anxious speculation about when its military would attack Holland, Luxembourg, Belgium, and France. By the end of the month France was on the verge of defeat, leaving Britain on its own. As the Roosevelt administration watched the war move across the map of Europe, it began to speak publicly in the rhetoric of military preparedness to mobilize the nation's citizens for the coming war. Roosevelt had begun a defense program immediately after Kristallnacht in November 1938, when Hitler forces invaded and destroyed Jewish homes, schools, hospitals, synagogues, and business centers. He had ordered the navy yards to run two or three shifts (Cook, *Eleanor Roosevelt,* v. 2, 570).

A national debate that had been growing over whether or not the United States should enter the war became even more intensive, developing violent extremes on both the political right and left. Public opinion was divided among such groups as interventionists, pacifists, Communists, Socialists, isolationists, American Firsters, Fascists, and Nazis. So the national context in which Bishop wrote from Key West harbor to describe the arrival of the navy to Moore was one fraught with sharp debate, for the Roosevelt interventionist narrative had not yet reached a point of public acceptance. According to the sympathetic Roosevelt scholar Joseph Lash, Roosevelt worried about his third-term presidential election during this time because public opinion polls showed that 83 percent of the voters opposed U.S. entry into the war, although a high percentage favored aid to England (242-243). Former *Washington Post* editor and publisher Katharine Graham recalls writing about antiwar, isolationist, and pacifist "propaganda groups and the American First Committee" as well as "Mrs. Roosevelt's . . . third term" about the same time (131).

What is particularly uncanny about Bishop's June 8, 1940, letter to Moore deploring the U.S. naval presence in Key West is the fact that her heightened anxieties anticipate by only two days two major turning points in the national war narrative and its accompanying cultural politics. On June 10, Roosevelt sent the clearest signal to date of the U.S. commitment to fight Fascism in a speech that effectively ended U.S. neutrality. In addition, MacLeish, then Librarian at the Library of Congress, published "The Irresponsibles" in *The New Republic*, criticizing writers like Ernest Hemingway "for having devalued the words and conceptions and slogans needed for high morale in war" (103-21).

Roosevelt's speech accomplished two major goals. First, it ended rhetorical neutrality on the war. Second, it introduced into the national World War II narrative a male war bonding convention. Roosevelt adapted French Premier Paul Reynaud's description of Italy's decision from a letter announcing that Italy had stabbed its neighbor in the back. Reynaud's rhetoric of neighborly and brotherly betrayal, according to historian Doris Kearns Goodwin, became a rallying cry for mobilization for the Allies when Roosevelt added it to a speech he gave in the United States: "On this tenth day of June, 1940, the hand that held the dagger has stuck it into the back of its neighbor" (68).

When Roosevelt decided to adapt Reynaud's image of neighborly and brotherly betrayal to condemn Italy, he also was working with a war discourse convention that he knew his audience would recognize. He was appropriating the weight of centuries of Western heroic and religious patriotic discourse about brotherly love and male bonding in the service of war that encouraged masculine sacrifice to save the honor of the nation (represented by the faithful waiting women, children, elderly, and others unable to fight). World War I propaganda had relied prominently upon it. As Fussell states in *The Great War and Modern Memory*, soldiers were depicted as both crucified Christ-figures and as boy-buddies in the manner of the adventure stories of G. A. Henty and H. Rider Haggard (119; 21). Owen draws the parallel between Christ and his soldiers in a well-known letter to Osbert Sitwell written in early July 1918:

> For 14 hours yesterday I was at work—teaching Christ to lift his cross by numbers, and how to adjust his crown; and to imagine the thirst until after the last halt. I attended his Supper to see that there were no complaints; and inspected his feet that they should be worthy of the nail. I see to it that he is dumb, and stands at attention before his accusers. With a piece of silver I buy him every day, and with maps I make him familiar with the topography of Golgotha. (Owen 562)

If Roosevelt had drawn upon the conventions of male bonding before the Great War, this appeal would have worked immediately. However, writers such as Hemingway had exposed them, calling their legitimacy into question. So MacLeish's condemnation of writers like Hemingway on the same day as Roosevelt's speech sent the message that writers were to stop approaching Hitler in terms of the last war with its vicious deceit and to consider that this new war was a "war that had to be fought" (*A Time to Speak* 103-121). MacLeish was calling male writers to arms, in essence, to unite behind male bonding conventions again on behalf of the interventionist narrative.

Popular advertising also supported this war convention, with explicit Christ-like depictions of white male soldiers. A March 1943 advertising announcement by the Magazine Publishers of America, for example, portrayed a Christ-soldier mobilizing citizens as brothers upon whom U.S. troops depended for their lives. Barbed wire depicted the "crown of thorns." A broken barbed wire and wooden fence made up the cross in the right corner of the ad. The soldier's left cupped hand stretched out in a Christ-like crucifixion pose, as shells dropped from the machine gun across the dead soldier's stomach. The ad also used biblical language. "By his deeds . . . measure yours" was the major slogan, as the ad exhorted civilian workers to work hard without complaining: "In the name of God and your fellow man, that is your job" (Roeder 14).

The male-bonding or boy-buddy ethic from the First World War continued throughout World War II, but some viewed it with ambivalence. According to Goodwin, Eleanor Roosevelt worried about Churchill's "'male tendency to romanticize war.'" Reporter Martha Gellhorn believed that Churchill enjoyed war, says Goodwin: "He loved the derring-do and rushing around. He got Roosevelt steamed up in his boy's book of adventure" (310). But not all of this romance was British. The U.S. military historian John Keegan describes two strains of the American romance with the airborne in his *Fields of Battle.* One strain was the boyish exaltation lifting America skyward, hence the romance with aviation heroes. It was not until the later war bombings of Dresden and then Japan that many, such as the poet Randall Jarrell in poems like "Eighth Air Force," "Losses," and "Burning of the Letters," began to discern a darker strain in this romance: the deadly payoff of airborne cargo (Goldensohn, "Randall Jarrell's War," 18-20).

Women's roles also demanded extensive attention from Roosevelt because of the Great War. World War I propaganda in the United States had directed its women on how to support its war efforts. Great War posters had shown women in the archetypal role of Penelope—as mothers, wives, neighbors, classmates, daughters, girlfriends, and family members watching the troops leave for war or waving goodbye to them with affection and support. Women were expected to knit and make bombs and sons for battle and functioned as life-givers and nurturers, conservers of national resources, and voices of support (Van Wienan 64; 154).

But women's role as patriotic Penelope also had become associated with the idea that women openly and aggressively sent men to their deaths. Women participated in the war's recruiting campaign by giving white feathers to men whom they felt were avoiding military service, thereby using shame to promote enlistment (Gullace, "White Feathers," 180).

In addition, major literary women like Virginia Woolf and Gertrude Stein linked the era's nationalistic war tensions to paternalism. Stein, for example, criticized memorably the excessive desire to "father" among the globe's leaders:

> There is too much fathering going on just now and there is no doubt about it fathers are depressing. Everybody nowadays is a father, there is father Mussolini and father Hitler and father Roosevelt and father Stalin and father Lewis and father Blum and father Franco is just commencing now and there are ever so many more ready to be one. (133)[5]

To counter these views, Roosevelt redefined the heroic and patriotic U.S. woman's role at the home front in the Second World War in January 1940. He designated the white heterosexual woman as the representation of U.S. democracy, placing her inside what historian Sonya Michel has described as the "discourse of the democratic family in World War II" (Higonnet 154). Roosevelt pronounced the family a "threshold of democracy, . . . a school for democratic life" as part of the nation's defense: "A succession of world events has shown us that our democracy must be strengthened at every point of strain or weakness" (Higonnet 155). As Leila Rupp has explained in her studies of women's war mobilization, this was how U.S. women were "to engage in deeds that partake of received notions of glory, honor, nobility, and civic virtues" (115). Ironically, however, they began extra war work inside and outside the home that often took them away from their family duties.

World War II media images supported Roosevelt's desired role for women by focusing on women as the faithful nation waiting for the soldiers, showing them sewing at home for the troops, participating in rationing campaigns, and working in defense plants. (Even before the U.S. entry into the war, U.S. women showed their support for the Allies by wearing British emblems [pins, ear studs, lapel jewelry] with the slogan "Bundles for Britain.") Later media during this war gradually exploited women's sexuality more explicitly than had Great War propaganda. The "democratic" woman represented by film star pinups like Betty Grable, the servicemen's favorite, conveyed the designated Penelope-like gender role for women waiting at home for their men with sexual glamour. Grable, the well-known wife of the jazz trumpeter Harry James, represented a combination of marital or sexual loyalty and motherhood (Westbrook 587–614).

Media imagery reinforced not only male and female home front roles but also family roles that reflect a homogeneous, upper-class white society rather than the diverse population of the nation. Paul Fussell points out in his study of World War II culture that readers of advertisements in such popular magazines as *Life, Look,* and *The Saturday Evening Post* in the years 1942 to 1945 would have surmised that the ideal Americans fighting the war and waiting at home for the soldiers were "nice" upper-middle-class Anglo-Saxon slim, tall blondes (*Wartime* 127). He goes on to say: "Notable is the absence of any feature which might be interpreted as Jewish, or Central European, or in any remote way 'colored' . . . in advertising, a medium where only ideal imagery can be allowed to enter. . . . In fiction or film, the GI might be Jewish or Italian, Polish or Hispanic or 'Colored'" (127–28).

While MacLeish called male writers to arms, Millay, one of the most popular poets of the era and a Vassar graduate and New Englander like Bishop, offered her poetic talents to the war effort and served as the model for women poets' propaganda role as "poets" to save "democracy" in World War II.[6] She was well acquainted with Hitler's war efforts through her husband's family in Europe. Fascist atrocities convinced her to reconsider her earlier pacifism, challenging her to weigh carefully how to oppose genocide, slave labor, territorial conquest, and totalitarianism. Millay sent a telegram to Roosevelt on December 27, 1940, pledging the continuation of her support of his interventionism, which had begun in June. In a separate telegram to his personal secretary Marguerite (Missy) LeHand on the same day, she reminded LeHand that she had given her a comb when they were both guests of French Ambassador William Bullitt. LeHand responded to Millay on January 2, 1941, indicating that she remembered her and that the president appreciated her thoughtfulness in writing very much (Papers of President Franklin D. Roosevelt, Franklin D. Roosevelt Library, Hyde Park). Millay was by no means alone in her political transformation. Other Americans had reconsidered their views in light of emerging war news and decided to support interventionism.

It is probably no accident, given her telegrams to Roosevelt and LeHand, that one day after the president's turning point speech and MacLeish's impassioned essay's publication, the June 11 issue of *The New*

York Times had carried Millay's poem, "Lines Written in Passion and in Deep Concern for England, France and My Own Country" under the headline "Isolationists Are Ridiculed Lest We Be Left to War Alone" with subheading "Edna St. Vincent Millay Paints Verse Picture of Tidal Waves of Troops Devouring Isles of Democracy." According to the news account, the poem was "given to the newspapers . . . that it might obtain an immediate audience" because Millay was "moved by the President's speech at Charlottesville and concerned over the tendency of some to regard this as Europe's war" (10).

Bishop was likely aware of Roosevelt's, MacLeish's, and Millay's activities. She had visited Hemingway, who admired the just-published "The Fish," for the first time on May 2, and met his wife Pauline and her sister Virginia (Millier 156). Shortly afterwards, on June 24, Hemingway retorted to MacLeish in *Time.*

Bishop's letter to Moore, dated September 1, 1940, reveals that the war news filled her with "frantic haste" and worry:

> . . . . I want to come to New York, but first I shall probably . . . see if I can't get something done that makes me feel better able to face my friends. The [war] news seems to fill me with such frantic haste and I am so worried about what may become of Key West. (*OA* 93)

Bishop's own anxieties about Fascism were pitched so high that only three days before *The New York Times*'s publication of Millay's interventionist poetry on October 20, 1940, she wrote Moore her well-known letter about her developing poem "Roosters," disturbed by her friend's attempt to edit it and change the way she wished to represent her wartime experience. In it she expressed her distress over the German takeovers in Finland and Norway as well as the pro-Franco German bombing of a Basque town during the Spanish Civil War and suggested that a bond existed between her own small Key West and these small towns. In addition to her overt denunciation of Fascism in the poem, she said that she also wanted to emphasize "the essential baseness of militarism," suggesting that she disagreed with militarism as a matter of general principle:

> I cherish my 'water-closet' and other sordidities because I want to emphasize the essential baseness of militarism. In the first part I was thinking of Key West, and also of those aerial views of dismal little towns in Finland and Norway, when the Germans took over, and their atmosphere of poverty. That's why . . . I want to keep 'tin rooster' instead of 'gold,' and not use 'fas-

tidious beds.' And for the same reason I want to keep as the title the rather contemptuous word ROOSTERS rather than the more classical THE COCK; and I want to repeat the 'gun-metal.' (I also had in mind the violent roosters Picasso did in connection with his *Guernica* picture.)

About the 'glass-headed pins': I felt the roosters to be placed here and there (by their various crowings) like the pins that point out war projects on a map. (*OA* 96)

Bishop's equation of Key West with the Nazi-occupied towns in Finland and Norway and the bombed Basque town is complicated. On one hand, she seems to identify Key West so completely with these communities that she projects the Nazi invasion and bombing of her own home. On the other hand, she seems to treat the U.S. Navy as though it were invading Key West to establish a military center at the expense of the civilians like Bishop living there. In any case the letter is highly emotional and defensive—as though Moore had trespassed not only on Bishop's literary expression, but on something even more important to her. Indeed, the images of the roosters evoked her Nova Scotian childhood home, Great Village, and the homesickness that she felt for this world when she moved to Massachusetts. Barry has pointed out that "a brief passage in an unfinished novel about her childhood in Great Village, written in the mid–1930s, contains a crowing rooster with his wives" ("Elizabeth Bishop and World War I," 108). As Bishop herself states in "A Country Mouse," her grandfather John Bishop, a U.S. immigrant from Prince Edward Island in Canada, bought her two hens and a rooster that thrilled her (30).

The tie between this letter, "Roosters," and the trauma of her Great War childhood is crucial. As recounted in her prose piece "The Country Mouse," written in 1960, she was brought in 1917 from the Nova Scotian family home of her permanently hospitalized mother to the United States to live with her deceased father's family. Her mother's final breakdown occurred because she thought that she was going to die for her country and that she was the cause of the war (Barry, "Elizabeth Bishop and World War I," 97).

As Dickie has correctly pointed out, this wartime move is highly significant for Bishop's attitude toward war: "the war was perhaps the only real link with her life in Nova Scotia" (104). Dickie goes on to state:

Her interest in different national styles of patriotism [resulting from her move] . . . inform her poetry. . . . Her attitude toward war may have been conditioned by her childhood sense of being an outsider, a non-patriot, a native of no country. (104-5)

In addition to all of this, and even more important, the war was both her last continuous early childhood link to her biological mother and surrogate mother, her grandmother, and the occasion of her rupture from them. While Bishop revisited Nova Scotia, she never lived there again.

Bishop writes in her memoir that her socialization into U.S. citizenship created a struggle within herself. She knew that she was expected to become loyal to the United States, but this legal expectation did not necessarily erase her feelings of affection for Nova Scotia and Canada, the only world she had known and loved, or her earlier indoctrination into songs of the British Empire and Canada and the pink-colored nations of the empire. To cope with her dilemma, she learned to hide and protect her double national identities, for such multiple allegiances seemed problematical in the Great War.

Bishop recalls vividly her struggle between nations in "The Country Mouse":

> [We] pledged allegiance to the flag and sang war songs. . . . I hated the songs, and most of all I hated saluting the flag. I would have refused if I had dared. In my Canadian schooling the year before, we had started every day with "God Save the King" and "The Maple Leaf Forever." Now I felt like a traitor. I wanted us to win the War, of course, but I didn't want to be an American. When I went home to lunch, I said so. Grandma was horrified; she almost wept. Shortly after, I was presented with a white card with an American flag in color at the top. All the stanzas of "Oh, say, can you see" were printed on it in dark blue letters. Every day I sat at Grandma's feet and attempted to recite this endless poem. . . . Most of the words made no sense at all . . .
>
> There were the war cartoons, several big books of them: German helmets and cut-off hands haunted us. (*Collected Prose* 26-28)

Bishop's story is important because it tells us that she experienced two major defining aspects of the Great War victory narrative in the United States: the promotion of visible signs of patriotism (i.e., singing the national anthem) and the use of demonizing propaganda about the enemy that frightened her. Her mastery of the gender conventions of the war before her arrival in Massachusetts is apparent from her account that she thought that a uniformed chauffeur in Boston was a "new kind of soldier" (16). Moreover, she knew that women were not supposed to discuss war because her aunt was not allowed to discuss the war cartoons about the helmets and cut-off hands (26).

Bishop's grandmother's "forced feeding" exercises in patriotism and citizenship behavior, which included compulsory recitation of the national anthem, may seem unduly harsh for such a young child in a new country. Her horror, tears, and severe disciplinary action provide, however, important insight into the complex civilian context accompanying the Great War and its victory narrative. Not everyone supported the U.S. effort in the war in the same way. Christopher Gibbs has argued that the greatest interventionist enthusiasm in the Great War was located in the metropolitan areas of the Northeast United States—exactly where Bishop then lived with her grandparents, who were major public leaders in Worcester (vii). Gibbs notes that several political leaders exploited the war situation and compromised civil liberties: "some members of the government set people up against each other . . . by encouraging people to spy on each other, by threatening, bribing, coercing people to work for the war" (134). Some leaders suppressed freedom of speech, harassed and imprisoned dissenters, and promoted political conformity, according to Van Wienen (19). Then after the war, U.S. Attorney General A. Mitchell Palmer conducted raids into civilian lives that inflamed tensions over civil liberties issues.

African American literary leaders were especially aware of civil liberty violations and racism both at home and abroad and spoke out while also supporting U.S. national goals. W. E. B. Dubois, for instance, wrote a *Crisis* editorial, "World War & the Color Line," in which he blamed the European conflict upon European colonizers and their shared history of the economic exploitation of non-European colonies: "Today civilized nations are fighting like mad dogs over the right to con and exploit . . . darker people" (Van Wienen 28-29). But the *Crisis* also constructed African American soldier-poets and military heroes who claimed the ideals of masculine heroism and patriotism (Van Wienen 141).

The war cartoons with the German helmets and cut-off hands, which Bishop's aunt could not discuss but which terrorized the young Elizabeth anyway, were actually forms of British and U.S. propaganda, according to Nicoletta Gullace. In order to gain support for the war, the national governments of both countries claimed that German soldiers cut off the feet, hands, or breasts of their victims. They consciously employed gendered violence—the image of a violated female sexuality—to justify their war policy ("Sexual Violence," 714-15; 747). In other words, British and U.S. women were seen as passive wards, needing protection from the savage German invaders.

In addition to experiencing the war as a child-observer with a new national identity, Bishop, as Sandra Barry has pointed out, "shared in the shock and grief" over this war's carnage, most specifically through the collision on December 9, 1917, of a French munitions ship and a Belgian relief ship in the Halifax, Nova Scotia, Harbor. The explosion killed nearly two thousand persons, injured many more thousands, and devastated the cities of Halifax and Dartmouth. Bishop's mother was a resident in the female ward of a hospital on the harbor, where all the windows shattered and the plastered walls and ceilings crumbled, traumatizing patients beyond recovery.

As Barry further notes, while Bishop's War World I–era poem "In the Waiting Room" published during the late Cold War does not refer overtly to this war catastrophe, such imagery as the volcanic eruption seems closely connected to it. Moreover, the date of the poem's events on February 5, 1918 was almost the two-month anniversary of the disaster; and the war relief effort from Massachusetts (because of its large-scale ties with Nova Scotia) was still continuing ("Elizabeth Bishop and World War I," 19-22;37).

But not all of the "child" versions of Bishop remember tragic memories or seems angry and confused. One "child" self expresses an innocence long lost—an awe and boastfulness over the Nova Scotian soldiers in the Great War, who wore kilts with tam-o'-shanters with thistles and other insignia (*Collected Prose* 28). This voice sometimes offers an incongruently awestruck impression of military regalia and theatrics in Bishop's poetry, underscoring the loss of innocence in war. So when Moore criticized "Roosters," she touched painfully upon Bishop's childhood trauma in the Great War as well as her growing anxieties about her civilian world in the Second World War.

Not surprisingly, Bishop pondered the rupture of civilian life during the war while Millay was featured prominently in *The New York Times Magazine* of October 20, 1940, with four war poems under a large etching of a road filled with traveling soldiers, horses, and cannons that were entitled "An Eclipse of the Sun Is Predicted," "The Old Men of Vichy," "Sonnet (Where does he walk, or sit and stir his tea)," and "Sonnet (How innocent of me and my dark pain)" (12). As "Roosters" appeared in *The New Repub-*

lic in April 1941, Bishop was presiding over major changes in her Key West life. Crane had decided to stay in New York City permanently because she was pursuing Billie Holiday and enjoying life as an impresario of the arts. After several trips back and forth between New York and Key West, she made a final break with Bishop (Fountain 84–87). Bishop became depressed and suicidal (Fountain 85–86).

Bishop rented their home to navy personnel, reporting on July 26 that the new tenants had come from the New London submarine base. She spent September and October in Brevard, North Carolina, and then went to New York to visit Crane. She returned to Key West in December after the bombing of Pearl Harbor to live with Marjorie Stevens, who worked as an accountant for the navy, on Margaret Street.

In a letter dated December 28, 1941 to Moore, Bishop indicates her anxieties about likely war evacuation, however necessary, and the ethics of the situation:

> . . . . I am rather depressed about Key West—and my house—just now [three weeks after Pearl Harbor attack]. The town is terribly overcrowded and noisy. . . . and not a bit like itself. It is one of those things one can't resent, of course, because it's all necessary, but I really feel that this is no place to be unless one is of some use. They are talking about evacuating the civilians. I don't believe they will, but still. . . . I haven't given up on the idea of South America. I'm not a bit sure of the ethics of it all—what do you think? (*OA* 104–105)

While Bishop worried about the naval evacuation of Key West civilians, Millay took center stage in 1942 as the national patriotic woman-poet. Her New Year's Day 1942 poem, "Not to be Spattered by His Blood (St. George Goes Forth to Slay the Dragon)," appeared under a large depiction of the mythical St. George and the evil dragon in *The New York Times Magazine* (10). Later in the year, Millay wrote *The Murder of Lidice*. It depicted the Nazi razing of the Czechoslovakian town of Lidice at the request of the Writers' War Board as part of an Allied attempt to memorialize the town so that it would not be completely erased from the Czech map or human memory, as the Nazis had intended. On October 19 and 20, 1942, it was broadcast coast-to-coast over NBC Radio with a cast headed by Alexander Woollcott before a radio studio audience of two thousand people at Radio City. It was then shortwaved in English, Spanish, and Portuguese to not only all of the continental United States but to continental Alaska, Spanish-Speaking Latin America and Brazil, Australia,

New Zealand, India, the British Isles, and the Middle East as well. At the end of the radio broadcast, Millay was brought to the platform, and a bound manuscript of the poem in both its original draft and final form was auctioned off for the benefit of Czechoslovakian relief.

Other promotional efforts quickly followed. Harper & Brothers published the complete text of the poetic drama in pamphlet form for 60 cents on October 20 to reach a mass readership. A large extract of the poem was published in the October 17 issue of *Life;* and a smaller extract appeared in the October 17 issue of *The Saturday Review of Literature.* Local churches, schools, and community groups throughout the country quickly pursued the poem for further local dramatic presentations. Due to popular request, the broadcast was repeated in January 1943. NBC's publicist Margaret Cuthbert sent the poetry manuscript to RKO Radio Pictures in the hope that it would be an idea for a motion picture, since the administration had turned heavily to the movie industry in its propaganda efforts. But RKO did not pursue it. Cuthbert was told that the studio was filming three anti-Nazi stories and would not have room for another (Millay, Margaret Cuthbert and Alice Blim Collection, Folder 12.4, VC).

The archival papers at Vassar of Cuthbert, a publicist at NBC at the time and personal friend of Millay, reveal the considerable public relations effort behind this Millay poem. Cuthbert was responsible not only for the national press coverage and national response already indicated but for urging NBC to present the poem (September 10, 1942, Folder 9.3, Millay, VC).[7] In a September 21, 1942 letter to Millay and her husband, Cuthbert indicated her relief at learning that NBC would present the poem and then outlined publicity efforts planned by the writers' war board, directing Millay to consider quoting from earlier poetry in *The New York Times* and to emphasize the danger she felt from the Axis powers (Folder 9.4, VC).

RKO publicity writer Joe Ransom was chosen for the Millay project publicity and the photographs of Millay taken at Steepletop, her home in Austerlitz, New York. The October 26, 1942, issue of *Newsweek* used a photo of Millay with a draft of the poetry manuscript in front of the fireplace (72). A photo of Millay standing with the poetry manuscript in front of the fireplace mantel in her home appeared with an excerpt of the poem in the October issue of *Life* (23).

Cuthbert seized every opportunity on behalf of the project, giving careful attention to such matters as broadcast date. She urged NBC, for instance, to consider a date near October 25 because Canada was to celebrate the naming of a town "Lidice" on October 25 and Roosevelt and MacKenzie King, prime minister of Canada, would speak. She thought the program would benefit from the accumulated interest of the public in the Canadian event. (September 21, 1942 letter, Folder 9.4, VC)

Millay became so identified with the voice of the nation at war that her poetry was an expected part of every major war event. Her poem "Thanksgiving, 1942," for example, appeared in the November 22, 1942, issue of *The New York Times Magazine* under a sketch depicting a turkey under attack from a vulture and continued onto the next page accompanied by photos of planes over Midway and soldiers in New Guinea (3–5). She wrote "Poem and Prayer for an Invading Army," which was broadcast by NBC and read by Ronald Colman during its twenty-four-hour coverage of the Allied invasion of Normandy on June 6, 1944.

In sharp contrast to Millay, who continued to commit herself and her poetry to the cause of the war for the rest of its duration from her longtime home in New York, Bishop struggled with the precariousness of civilian life in a major military installation on the home front. Her earlier concerns about civilian evacuation, for example, indicate U.S. government anxieties about the population's safety in case of attack, a realistic assessment given Key West's importance in protecting the mainland as well as monitoring the Caribbean, Central America, and South America for German submarines. The navy built military housing in the field across from Bishop's White Street house (Fountain 88).

As Bishop was learning, military protection also can result in the displacement of the civilian population and the general disruption of their lives in the immediate area. On April 2, 1942, she wrote Charlotte Russell about her anger over the military appropriations of civilian Key West and her political action against it. She and Pauline Hemingway were conducting a campaign to wire Senator Claude Pepper about the naval bulldozing of block upon block of homes. Bishop found that some people were receiving only a day's warning to move from their homes and that African Americans were sleeping in cars and vacant lots. Such expression of anger and political mobilization reveals the extent to which she was seriously distressed. In the letter she condemned not only the navy's effects on her public world in Key West but also its impact on her private life. She and her lover Marjorie Stevens were planning to evacuate and stay in Mexico for perhaps the rest of the war. Indicating that she did not want to be "unpatriotic" about it, Bishop felt that the naval action would reduce Key West to a naval base, bars, and cheap apartments and was unnecessary (*OA* 106–107).

So the naval installation with its constant sound of airplanes, the daily noise from dynamiting, bulldozing, and building, the nightly blackouts, and the overcrowding and homelessness seemed too overwhelming to Bishop and Stevens, and they went to Mexico and stayed from April into the fall of 1942 (*OA* 106-7; Fountain 88). During this time, Bishop corresponded with the husband of her good friend Loren MacIver, Lloyd Frankenberg, who as a conscientious objector during the war had been sent to a special camp. She had hoped the camp would not be too difficult and offered to send such gifts as books and cigarettes to him (Folder 4.4, VC). He had left her with a copy of his draft board document (now in her archives at Vassar) stating his reasons for conscientious objection with the help of the War Resisters League. In the document Frankenberg explained his antiwar views in general, relying heavily upon his religious training, his interpretation of Ghandi's nonviolence, the poetry of Wilfred Owen and other Great War British poets, Stephen Crane's *The Red Badge of Courage,* the film *All Quiet on the Western Front,* Rainer Maria Rilke's *Wartime Letters,* Aldous Huxley's "What Are You Going To Do About It? The Case for Constructive Peace," and his own poetry (Folder 4.4, VC). He explained at length that he felt that his nonparticipation in any war was fitting tribute to Owen's poetry because the writing had come directly out of Owen's warfront experience.

In a letter to Frankenberg dated June 29, 1942, Bishop responded to his views and deplored the fact that poetry had been brought into the justification:

> . . . . In general you prophesied awfully well . . . I've just re-read all of Owen this morning and there are several points there I'd like to ask you about. . . . I only wish poetry hadn't had to be brought in at all—but then I suppose there's no use in trying to protect it, either. (*OA* 112)

Frankenberg wrote her back on September 17, 1943, indicating that he did not think that poetry was automatically a part of a pacifist belief system because he felt that there was good poetry glorifying war as well as denouncing it (Folder 4.4, VC). Then he outlined ideas for a poetry anthology about poetry and war. He pointed out that he did not know of any antiwar poems until Stephen Crane's "War Is Kind," which indicated that pacifist poetry might be related to the advent of modern war in the U.S. Civil War with its large-scale impact on the civilian population. He speculated that the Great War poetry fell into two large segments, early idealization and later disillusionment, whereas World War II began with the disillusionment expressed in W. H. Auden's "The Double Man," which compared the approach of war to a cheap detective story, and he predicted that the major pacifist poetry of the war might come out of the army itself.

No record of Bishop's response to Frankenberg's intense views has been discovered. But it is perhaps no coincidence that she became silent in her poetry while others continued to write and to publish about the war. She had not wanted poetry to be used as an argument to justify one's beliefs about war. In addition, Frankenberg had raised the problematical position that women writing about the war faced by indicating that Owen's war-front experience was the ultimate source for good poetry about a war, a view he underscored by suggesting that the best pacifist poetry might come from the army. Women were not at risk for warfront duty, so finding a position from which to write and be taken seriously on the subject of war was difficult. Bishop's understanding of World War II came directly from her firsthand experience of watching Key West prepare to defend the nation and being dislodged from a peaceful, privileged civilian life and confronted with the daily reality of the equivalent of martial law as Key West was transformed into a major naval base. So unlike women poets on the mainland like Millay, Moore, Rukeyser, and Gwendolyn Brooks, Bishop found herself in a unique position that was neither like theirs nor like the men's, but in which complaint would be viewed as a blatant lack of patriotism.

Frankenberg's letter also indicated that he hoped that Bishop would winter in New York and that he might see her during a week's furlough at Thanksgiving. Bishop had visited New York in 1942 and met her later Brazilian companion Lota de Macedo Soares during this stay. Frankenberg's note is important because it indicates that Bishop was hoping to escape again from Key West, finding it no longer congenial.

Since Bishop's visit also came shortly after Millay had presented *The Murder of Lidice* and published her Thanksgiving poem for the armed services, she likely found herself weighing the cultural politics. While Millay's war efforts increased her visibility and popularity with the general American public, questions about the writing's poetic merits had surfaced as well. *The Murder of Lidice* was especially controversial. *The New York Times* reviewer John Hutchens, for example, commented: "How 'The Murder of Lidice' will rank with the body of her work is, for the moment, beside the point. . . . Not a great poem, not her best poem, but one which finely serves the time, the medium and the intention" (12). Hutchens's view, echoed by others, is prescient about the literary fate of Millay. By the next year, 1944, her reputation was waning: "[T]he greatest insult you can offer any young woman poet in this country is to warn her that she be the Edna Millay of her generation . . . ," wrote Winfield Townley Scott in *Poetry* (335). After the war in 1948 Millay told Edmund Wilson that it had been a "mistake" to write her poetry even if for morale, although she had announced earlier during the war that she recognized that she was consciously choos-ing to sacrifice her poetry to write propaganda as a moral imperative in the fight against Hitler (Edel 290).

But Bishop's continued poetic silence did not mean that she ignored the war. Marjorie Stevens returned to Key West from Mexico and corre-sponded regularly with Bishop while she visited New York, revealing that Bishop continued to follow the war intensely. In an undated letter during this time, Stevens agreed with Bishop that the liberation of Paris was won-derful news as were the incoming reports about the minimal damage to the city, much less than what London had experienced. She went on to cite the liberation as having profound psychological meaning and found signifi-cance in the fact that the French had fought for their city as well. Yet Stevens also is very guarded in the letter, explaining that she could say much more in conversation but hesitated even in a private letter to Bishop to write all that she might like, an indication that she was aware that her mail was subject to postal inspection because it came from Key West (Folder 20.8, VC).

In a letter dated November 12 and 14, 1942, Stevens reported a conver-sation with a coffee businessman about the course of the war to Bishop, again indicating that Bishop was interested in both news and informal assessments of the war. Stevens had found the man's comforting commen-tary unusual because in a military center like Key West with everyone and nearly everything "betraying the 'effects' of the war," no one talked openly about the war itself. He had appeared to her to be rather optimistic about the fact that the United States had finally severed ties with Vichy, that it would likely confiscate and use French boats now at Martinique, and that attacks on U.S. shipping would slow down because a second front had been opened in Europe (Folder 20.8, VC).

Although Bishop did not publish any poetry in 1943, she worked on "Songs for a Colored Singer" for both Crane's lover and her own friend Billie Holiday. When Moore published "In Distrust of Merits" in 1943, Bishop wrote on July 15 that she had been "overawed" into two months of silence by it (*OA* 113). In August she attempted to work in a defense job in optics in Key West. But she quickly received an honorable discharge because the work affected her eyes and made her seasick. The cleaning acids gave her eczema. So after five days she left. In a letter to Moore dated September 1, 1943, she said that the optical defense job had depressed her (Keller, "Words," 410). But by October Bishop had completed the poem for Holiday and sent it to Moore.

In 1944 Bishop was back in New York, with Stevens begging her to return to Key West for her health. The major turning point in the war, the Battle of Normandy, took place on June 6. For Bishop, September was a breakthrough month in her poetry career with the publication of "Songs for a Colored Singer" published in *Partisan Review.* Jean Pedrick invited her on the basis of the poem to submit her poetry manuscript for the first annual Houghton Mifflin poetry prize fellowship, resulting in the publication of her first poetry collection (Millier 174).

Bishop clearly was anxious about the cultural politics. She wondered how the poetry world and her reading public would judge her absence from the arena of war poetry and felt compelled to address the way that she contrasted with Millay or even Moore, who were both very much in the limelight. In a letter dated January 22, 1945, she asked her publisher Ferris Greenslet at Houghton Mifflin to explain her situation when it published *North & South:*

> The fact that none of these poems deal directly with the war, at a time when so much war poetry is being published, will, I am afraid, leave me open to reproach. The chief reason is simply that I work very slowly. But I think it would help some if a note to the effect that most of the poems had been written, or begun, at least, before 1941, could be inserted at the beginning, say just after the acknowledgments. I'll enclose a sheet with the acknowledgments and such a note, to see what you think. (*OA* 26)

It is ironic that Bishop seems to indicate here that *North & South* contained little war poetry, especially since critics began reading its war messages with Bogan as soon as it was published and when it contained one of the major poems about the war, "Roosters," along with a second major work not sufficiently appreciated as a later World War II poem, "Songs for a Colored Singer." One hears, however, in the letter her discomfort over her differing wartime experience with that of Millay, or even her friend Moore.

It is difficult to understand fully why Bishop wrote and published so little during the war because poets continued to register their wide-ranging views on the war effort, so she need not have worried about fitting into only one mold, or following Millay's model exclusively. Her mentor and friend Moore was actively publishing, as were Brooks and Rukeyser, who criticized the shortcomings of both Fascist and liberal militarism.[8] Conscientious objectors and other antiwar and pacifist proponents could be found on all sides of the war question. The issue of cultural politics and women poets' roles may explain some of Bishop's silence; and so may her unique witnessing of war's preparations in a major military center in contrast to the other poets' experiences. Certainly the fact that she felt it necessary to leave Key West for extended periods of time during the war suggests that the disruption of civilian life in a military base may be accompanied by a similar rupture in language and writing. In addition, Stevens's letter indicating her awareness that her missive might be read by a postal inspector reveals the reality of wartime surveillance and censorship.

The laments and anger in her letters during this period seem unusually strong, even excessive, for Bishop, who has for so long been read as a model of emotional control and balance. This high emotion fills not only "Roosters," but also "Songs for a Colored Singer"—the two major poetic wartime statements from Bishop that we will read in the next chapter.

In addition to the war traumas, one can also hear in these letters from Key West the "version" of Bishop who does not wish to have her comfortable world of privilege disrupted by war. She feared the loss of not only comfort and privilege but the physical and inner space for writing provided by this privilege: the poor, racially segregated Key West world she was depicting in both her poetry and her sketching and painting.[9]

In poems like "Jerónimo's House" and "Cootchie" she represents the complex multicultural race- and class-oppressed local cultures of Key West and in this respect refuses to follow the dominant cultural tendency of the era to ignore the existence of difference. However, she also domesticates and/or primitivizes racial difference and "otherness," reifying her own privilege and reproducing the era's stereotypes.[10] Whether depicting this world in terms of hominy grits, the Spanish flamenco on the radio at Jerónimo's house, or the suicide of Miss Lula's African American servant Cootchie who ate her food at the sink while Miss Lula ate at the dining table, Bishop offers a contradictory mix of empathy and admiration with a limited ability to depict cultural difference on a level playing field (*CP* 34, 46).

So while Bishop generally wrote and published slowly, one often senses a near-paralysis at work in "moments" of unresolved conflict and stress like the Second World War. Her silence between "Roosters" and "Songs for a Colored Singer" cannot be ignored. It may have offered a carefully chosen strategy of subversion to distance herself from the problematics of poetry and war politics. It may indicate her support of the war since she had not openly written antiwar poetry after the U.S. entry into the war, she had attempted defense work, and she did not wish to be "un-patriotic" about leaving Key West. It also may signal layers of quasi-visible anxieties about civil liberties and military policing during wartime and quasi-(in)visible resistance originating in childhood war trauma, the self-centeredness of privilege, a desire to protect her private life, and literary marketplace ambitions. No matter how one reads the silence, however, it cannot be seen as simply a matter of either marketplace anxiety or antimilitarist conscience. The silence is much more complex than that. The next chapter will examine "Roosters" and "Songs for a Colored Singer" to consider the confounding war politics that they illuminate.

Chapter 4 ⟜

BISHOP'S VISIONS OF "UNWANTED LOVE, CONCEIT, AND WAR"

W hen the speaker looks out the "gun-metal blue" bedroom window in Bishop's pre–Pearl Harbor poem "Roosters," the sun "climbs in":

> following 'to see the end,'
> faithful as enemy, or friend. (*CP* 39)

This poem, written in tercets, offers evidence for both the anti-Fascist "version" as well as the generally antimilitarist "versions" of Bishop, but also for the Bishop who worried about the home front. Bishop's well-known letter about the poem to Moore cited in the last chapter indicates that she condemned the Nazi takeovers in Finland and Norway and the pro-Franco German bombing of a Basque town, perhaps Guernica itself, and connected her own Key West to the many small communities there. But she also had said that she denounced the "essential baseness of militarism." Her other letters during this time reveal her anxieties about the effect of the U.S. naval presence in Key West in her own life and civilian life in general.

At times she seems to hold the navy more responsible for her uncomfortable situation than the military aggression of the Axis powers of Germany, Italy, and Japan. This chapter's readings of both "Roosters" and "Songs for a Colored Singer" construct "versions" of Bishop that combine the personal with her public politics of anti-Fascism, general antimilitarism, and questions about the national World War II–era home-front construction of nation, war, culture, sexuality, gender, class, ethnicity, and race.

Bishop's condemnation of both Fascism and the principle of militarism is reflected in the construction of the speaker in the first section of the poem. This speaker—depicting a courtly love scenario between the hens and roosters and a male rivalry ritual among the roosters—has an unspecified national, sexual, gender, class, racial, and ethnic identity. Moreover, the speaker uses a personal "we" at a "gun-metal blue" bedroom window to tell us about the allegorical military invasion scene underway in the first light of dawn:

> At four o'clock
> in the gun-metal blue dark
> we hear the first crow of the first cock
>
> just below
> the gun-metal blue window
> and immediately there is an echo
>
> off in the distance,
> then one from the backyard fence,
> then one, with horrible insistence,
>
> grates like a wet match
> from the broccoli patch,
> flares, and all over town begins to catch. (*CP* 35)

The "first crow" of the cock results in an echo, then more "horrible insistence" that "flares" and "all over town begins to catch" like a fire, reminding one of guns, bombs, and as Spiegelman points out, military fanfare (157). Indeed, the passage seems especially to mark the introduction of *blitzkrieg,* "lightning war," from the use of Nazi bombers in the Spanish Civil War. On April 26, 1937, Guernica was the first open city to be bombed from the air without warning. The four-hour attack killed 1,654 people and wounded 889 in a town of seven thousand (Cook, *Eleanor Roosevelt,* v. 2, 444, 452).

This language also seems to place us as readers on a battlefield at dawn in some Great War soldier's writing as well as the official Nazi takeover of Paris on June 14, 1940. As Fussell explains about this kind of war writing, "When a participant in the war wants an ironic effect, a conventional way to achieve one is simply to juxtapose a sunrise or sunset with the unlovely physical details of the war that man has made" (*The Great War and Modern*

Memory 55). In addition, however, war's realities often began at dawn; and merely reporting them, rather than fictionalizing them, achieves this same effect. At dawn on June 14, for instance, Nazi troops arrived in Paris and awakened its citizens with loudspeakers warning that any hostile actions or demonstrations against the army would be punished by death (Goodwin 320).

But this poem is not supposed to be set in a militarized zone at all. It is supposedly set in civilian Key West, Florida. Bishop told the poet May Swenson about the poem in a letter dated February 18, 1956: ". . . . I started it and wrote all the beginning, and bits here and there . . . at 4 or 5 a.m. in the back yard in Key West, with the roosters carrying on just as I said" (*OA* 316). What she did not add is that naval housing in Key West went up in the field across from her 624 White Street house so that the war literally sprang up in her backyard and nearly took her own home (Fountain 88). Indeed, she rented her home to navy personnel.

By bringing the language of the battlefield into her personal as well as the more generic civilian farm world of Key West here, Bishop exposes the reality that battlefields are civilian worlds, too. Moreover, the battlefield of Key West is not different from the German-occupied zones of Norway and Finland, the war-torn world of Pablo Picasso's *Guernica,* or Paris. She draws attention, then, to the reality that World War II was not just a war "over there," but a war in the nation's "back yard" affecting U.S. civilians. In addition, she expresses anxieties about the militarization of civilian Key West. Just as she offers an emotionally charged, blurred analysis about whether this militarization results from the navy itself or from Axis aggression in her letters, so she wavers between the two here. In reality Axis aggression was linked to the naval installation, but of course, the navy also acted on its own initiative as well and not just reactively.

Bishop's decision to set "Roosters" in rural Key West and to use such a nonspecific speaker foregrounds more than her concerns about Nazism and militarism as a whole. It questions what constituted the home front United States that needed protection. The period's stereotypical "democratic family" was white and rural, or pastoral. A frontier or farming, small-town image legitimized the nation's victory culture with its depiction of the settlement process of the United States.[1] This image was both a cultural representation of the nation unifying all citizens regardless of actual social positioning—and a reality of life for some Americans. Popular interwar films of the period frequently focused on rural and small town worlds in both comedies and dramas—for instance, *Mr. Smith Goes to Washington* and

Meet John Doe. The major artistic movement of regionalism popularized a rural version of the United States in paintings by such artists as Thomas Hart Benton and Grant Wood.

Bishop's firsthand experience beginning in childhood with the "white" ideal focused on the sharp class distinctions existing between middle- to upper-class Anglo-Saxons and those "other whites," including Irish, Swedes, Germans, and so forth, some of whom lived in rural, farming, and small-town settings. In her memoir "The Country Mouse," Bishop wrote that she believed that her deceased father's upper-class family in Worcester, Massachusetts, thought that they were saving her from poverty and bare feet by demanding that she move from her mother's family in rural Nova Scotia. She admitted that she never felt secure in the Worcester upper-class homestead (*Collected Prose* 32).

While the national construction of the "democratic family" was white, Bishop's rural farm setting and speaker in the poem draw attention to gender, racial, and ethnic struggles within the nation that were being denied. The white male farmer may have symbolized America to some citizens, but in reality farms also were owned and/or managed by women farmers. African Americans and other ethnic groups such as Native Americans, Asian Americans, and Latinos also worked the soil and identified with the farm. Individual economic relationships to the land differed, with ownership belonging predominantly to whites. But workers from all social groups worked the land for their wages and fed themselves from tilled private house gardens and chickens raised in the backyard.

While all of these "farmers" are silenced or masked over by the dominant image of the white male farmer stereotype of the period, Bishop's personal speaker grows into a communal speaker with the use of "we" and such images of poverty as the "water closet" and "tin roosters," suggesting a more inclusive "democratic family." Bishop's interest here reflects her explorations of Key West's racially segregated, class-stratified, but heterogeneous, cosmopolitan Caribbean society of U.S. and European whites, African Americans, South Americans, Mexicans, and Cubans.

Bishop's gesture of inclusiveness is quite complex. The poem's "we" in line three refers to the couple or more than one sleeper sleeping behind the "gun-metal blue window." The "we" is then broadened in the phrase "our beds," linking the second reference to the first but now incorporating a wider community of sleepers. "Our churches" makes it, potentially at least, a community of worshippers, and "our houses," of home-dwellers. With the arrival of the roosters screaming, "This is where I live," the poem shifts between "you" and the sleepy "us" who are awakened by them. The final first-person plural in the poem refers to "our chanticleer," as the poem transforms the tin rooster overlooking the churches to the chanticleer in telling the story of Peter's betrayal of Christ in the second half of the poem. The transition to "our chanticleer" also rounds out the communal "we" to include not only the Key West community and, by extension, the home front, but also the reader of the poem, implicating "us" all in a sense of potential guilt, sin, or betrayal. Yet while the "we" seems all-encompassing, the biographical facts of Bishop's female and possibly male lovers suggest that a community of "outsiders" coexists within the broader general community, a group at risk under the roosters' rule because of homophobia in the United States and Germany.[2]

While Bishop attacks the invading roosters, she also lays blame for the siege on the domesticated front, the hens in the poem. In the "dropping-plastered" henhouse the speaker says that the "rustling wives admire" the cruel roosters with "green-gold medals." As Bishop's speaker points out, however, the "wives" do not seem to act freely:

> . . . . rustling wives admire,
> the roosters . . .
> planned to command and terrorize the rest,
> the many wives. (*CP* 35)

The "wives" in "Roosters" are not rewarded for their faithfulness to their rooster-dictators, or, as Bonnie Costello puts it, female submission to male arrogance (65).

In addition, because of the anti-Fascist and antimilitarist double narrative in the poem, it is not clear whether Bishop is more concerned with women's or home front complicity with Fascism or war in general, or with women's or home front victimization at the hands of aggressors, or both. Either way, or both ways, her wives are "dead," civilian victims of the battle:

> He is flung
> on the gray ash-heap, lies in dung
>
> with his dead wives
> with open, bloody eyes . . . (*CP* 37)

Not only do the hens live in continual danger, but they are subjected to abuse while they live. They are alternately rewarded and punished—"courted and despised." Whether as civilian supporters of Fascism or war in general, or as victims of Fascism or enemy aggression in general, women, and by extension the home front, in Bishop's poem suffer cruel fates.

World War I provides historical context for understanding this. Writings about even patriotic Allied women in the Great War indicate that much anger was directed at the very women who followed national directives for their role as citizens during wartime. As Sandra Gilbert's analysis of women's treatment in this war's propaganda and private writings points out, "wives" were ordered to acquiesce to militarism and support it, symbolizing the nation that the soldiers were to defend. Paradoxically, the soldiers saw them as responsible for the deaths of soldiers (197-226). Robert Graves, for example, reprinted "a famous piece of propaganda in the form of a letter from a 'little mother' who thinks women should gladly 'pass on the human ammunition' of sons" to the nation for its military (209). As we have discussed, British women participated actively in recruiting campaigns, "wielding the language of sexual shame to coerce young men into military service" as they distributed the dreaded symbol of effeminacy, "white feathers," to nonenlisted men (Gullace 180-182). Thus women, through national directives, were employed to define male roles as militaristic in order to serve national interests (183).

Bishop reinforces her warning to women about the dangers to them from Fascism and other forms of militarism by questioning the actions of the roosters. The roosters have "cruel feet" and "glare with stupid eyes." They command and terrorize—gloating over everyone under their control, mapping out their newly acquired territories, screaming at each other—with their "senseless order" about "how to live." Moreover, they are not what they appear to be.

The poem's speaker who represents "us" then confronts the roosters' legal and discursive authority, aroused by the suspicion that these roosters hide a duplicitous history behind their bravado. They expect acquiescence to death when they themselves have struggled against it. The speaker tells us that they resisted their own sacrifice to war gods in ancient Greek military culture. The authoritarian roosters are not invincible, nor are they omnipotent, in spite of their attempts to terrorize the masses into believing this. Their "concealed" history reveals that they are sacrificial victims in militarism. The speaker asks:

> what right have you to give
> commands and tell us how to live,

cry "Here!" and "Here!"
and wake us here where are
unwanted love, conceit and war? (*CP* 36)

The cry of "Here!" twice followed on the next line by "here" supports the poem's meaning, for it sounds like "hear" as well as the German "Herr." Spiegelman describes the roosters as exhibiting "lunatic, pseudo-heroic fighting swagger" (157).

This sound-play is further supported by the visual play of the only five exclamation points in the poem in these eleven lines of rooster cries. The exclamations remind the reader of footprints of combat boots in this context as each rooster marks out the "here" of his territory. The link to Nazism is apparent since the boots with the uniform were a major feature, so much so that the expression "black boot" in the work of such later poets as Sylvia Plath was read as shorthand for Nazism.

This use of exclamation points is reminiscent of Woolf's *Three Guineas* and its description:"loud of voice, hard of fist, childishly intent upon scoring the floor of the earth with chalk marks" (105, 109):

> A rooster gloats
> over our beds . . .

> making sallies
> from all the muddy alleys
> marking out maps like Rand McNally's:

> glass-headed pins,
> oil-golds and copper greens . . . (*CP* 36)

Over the Key West civilians' beds and the henhouses, each rooster screams "This is where I live!"

The repetition of the "here" with the exclamation points seems to reenact the opening scene in the poem where "there is an echo" of the "first crow" that repeats and grows larger until the town is up in flares. Only now the identity of the swaggering, noisy roosters is more Nazi. Indeed Katharine Graham compared a Hitler speech to a zoo when she listened to a broadcast in the late 1930s:"the broadcast sounded a little bit as though you had gotten the zoo by mistake—that rasping voice punctuated by roars that sounded like a pack of insane animals" (101).

The poem's frenzy of "marking out maps like Rand McNally's" reflects provocatively upon the role of mapping in the war, a mapping often represented by both land and women (the feminized home front). The war has been blamed generally on the remapping of territory in the World War I treaty. In addition, the aggressive mapping of Nazi military campaigns left everyone breathless.

But Bishop seems equally concerned with what this means for the feminized sphere of the nation's "democratic family." Her image is indeed an uncanny allegorical denouncement of such national moves as Roosevelt's appropriation of a previously female civilian space within the White House for his war room—or her own Key West home. Pacific and Atlantic maps covered the walls of the war room and replaced the women's coat hooks, according to Goodwin (310). Different-shaped pins designated different types of ships. Special pins tracked the locations of Churchill, Roosevelt, and Stalin (310-11). A symbolic space for the "democratic woman" in the "democratic family" at the nation's White House—and in Key West—thus was eradicated in favor of the needs of war.

In the poem itself, Bishop's mapping images draw together the conquest of the various roosters' own hen-civilians as well as the capture of "other" (enemy) hen-civilians. Bishop seems especially aware of a heterosexist power dynamic with male dominance over the feminine/civilian in the nation's World War II narrative. The roosters claim the henhouses and the hens inside them for their own in a menacing gesture suggesting spoilage and rape:

> A rooster gloats
> over our beds (*CP* 36)

This feminine/civilian linguistic and ideological slippage is a major characteristic of the war that distinguishes it from the nationalist struggles of the Great War. According to Susan Gubar, cultural historians have noted that Fascism and Nazism also seem to have regarded leadership as sexual mastery over the feminized masses (Higonnet 230). Since women make up most, but not all, of the civilian masses, feminized masses refers not only to women but to all civilians (children, the elderly, disabled, and so on). World War II thus had a much more definitive heterosexual struggle to it, whether defined as male military leadership over women or male military leadership over civilians. Clearly masculinity during the war was defined as heterosexual soldier, and the civilian was seen as a heterosexual female.

Sexism also played a role in mapping within the U.S. military during the Second World War. Actual mapreading classes in the U.S. military used pin-ups of glamorous and heterosexually provocative female movie stars like Betty Grable—in shirt only with exposed legs—to teach recruits how to read maps (Gubar 239). Women were transformed completely into hetero-sexual objects: the legs might map one bombing site; the breasts, friendly protected targets. Heterosexual women's bodies and body parts were thus appropriated not only for their procreative value but for their heterosexual allure to map out both the enemy's and one's own civilian territory or geography. Male soldiers were thus trained to "use" women's bodies in order to distinguish between friend and foe and to stay alive.

It is not surprising, then, that Bishop objects strenuously to sexist skew-ering of the female/civilian body and human vision. But this militarist manipulation did not stop with the military training. It extended to civil-ians as well. Roosevelt understood that most U.S. citizens did not know world geography, recounts Goodwin. Before his first "fireside chat" on Feb-ruary 23 after his Pearl Harbor speech, he asked his radio listeners to buy maps so that he could explain the Allied cause around the world to them. More than 61 million adults (nearly 80 percent of the total possible adult audience) listened to this speech, and many had their Rand-McNallies and other maps spread before them as Roosevelt explained each battle situation (319). Orders for *National Geographic* maps increased 600 percent (83). Pop-ular films, at the suggestion of the administration, also helped teach Amer-ican civilians the war's geography as well. Movies like *Casablanca* opened with maps to orient their viewers to the films' settings.

This "fatherly" education in maps and geography was hardly "innocent" or "neutral." Roosevelt wanted his audiences to understand where the troops were fighting and struggling and where they were winning. This means that civilians, like combatants, were taught to see the world through the binary vision of friend versus enemy. "Friendly" territories were to be spared and saved; "enemy" lands invaded. Jean Bethke Elshtain's studies of war imagery are relevant here for explaining this vision further. She writes that it "means seeing everything as existing in a state of extreme, Manichaean reduction, which erases all intermediate hues . . . and limits everything to . . . the primordial struggle of two forces—good and evil" (256).

The poem's speaker and the others in their Key West homes do not want to be "courted and despised" like the hens by the roosters' regimes of "unwanted love, conceit, and war." They want to be able to discern the duplicity behind their rhetoric. Certainly conceit means arrogance here, for this trait is generally associated with roosters. But "conceit" also refers to metaphor and figurative language. So it is reasonable to suggest as well that the word carries at least a double meaning: arrogance and the language of duplicity, both "unwanted" characteristics, in Jacqueline Brogan's words, of "phallocentric dominance," in the poem's speaker's view ("Perversity" 42). Moreover, "conceit" also suggests Fascism's arrogance, as well as other aggressive militarism's arrogance, in trying to remap the world through discourse. In any case, the poem wishes to rebuff the spread of "conceit."

The section of the poem following this outburst against the authority of the military state brings "unwanted love, conceit and war" even more directly to the speaker's bedroom window. "Virile" roosters with "vulgar beauty" attack one another, and "torn-out bloodied feathers drift down" (37). The dead hero ends in the ash-heap with his "dead wives" while "metallic feather," which Kathleen Brogan points out evokes warplane imagery, "oxidize" (63). The reader is left with the haunting juxtaposed double image of the rooster as both victimizer and victim: the terrorizing medal-chested rooster with "torn-out bloodied feathers" lying "in dung."

This double image in turn is complicated by a childlike mesmerization just before it, describing the flying, fighting roosters with "the crown of red / . . . on your little head." This child's voice creates the effect of dangerous innocence, for the child fails to recognize the deadliness of the scene, as well as corrupted innocence, for children are to be protected from such danger. In addition, the child seems to want to recognize the humanity—"little head"—behind the terrifying assailants. Just as easily, however, the adult narrator could be passing judgment on the roosters through the child by juxtaposition of human goodness and the evils of war.

Bishop offers in this depiction a cultural representation of war's mental, psychological, cultural, and physical injuries. Because the cockfight was an image familiar to many at this time either from their spectatorship at an actual cockfight or from popular culture, mass media, and literature, Bishop could expect that her readers would relate quickly to the roosters' injuries. This kind of representation of injury, explains war theorist Elaine Scarry, is too often omitted in official discourses of war and militarism and replaced by sanitized representations of whole human bodies as though injury, mutilation, and hurt, which are war's intent, do not exist (1, 20). World War II was no exception. Fussell reports that during the Great War the rhetoric of euphemism used by the military authorities and news reporters as well as the "stoical reticence" by the soldier-writers themselves combined with censorship to create a language that conveyed very little of war's realities

(174-90). He writes: "It was perhaps the first time in history that official policy produced events so shocking, bizarre, and stomach-turning that the events had to be tidied up for presentation to a highly literate mass population" (*The Great War & Modern Memory* 178).

This practice extended into World War II. George Roeder, in his study of World War II censorship, found that censorship of photographs extended to soldiers maimed in combat, shell-shocked GI's, soldiers killed in jeep accidents, and victims of Allied bombing raids and U.S. chemical warfare experiments (3). Although writers like Jarrell, Norman Mailer, William Styron, and Joseph Heller challenged the sanitized imagery early and late 1940s film noir addresses it indirectly, this depiction of the war has only recently been challenged in national visual popular culture with the Steven Spielberg film *Saving Private Ryan*—more than fifty years after the war.[3]

With the image of the rooster-hero and his dead wives in a mass war grave beneath the speaker's window, "Roosters" reveals that the promise of heroic mourning and commemoration ritual to honor both the war dead and their survivors is reduced to "ashes."

Yet Bishop is not finished with her rhetorical interrogation of Fascism and other virulent forms of militarism in the poem. After this image of mass war dead, the poem moves fully into the speaker's imagination shared with the reader and the second section of the poem. Ever since the poem was published originally in *The New Republic*, a space has been placed between the roosters' allegory and the Christian myth of the second part of the poem. While the two sections definitely offer two different kinds of narrative or story, they are unified by the transformation of the tin rooster above the churches into "our" chanticleer as the poem critiques the two major Anglo-American war conventions of courtly love and Christian male brotherhood. The space marks a transition between the two halves as the "dead wives" in the burial ash-heap with the vanquished rooster are metamorphosed into the "Magdalen / whose sin was of the flesh alone" and therefore are less guilty than the roosters.

But a blank space in a text also is a kind of language that deserves more attention than we have given it so far. Is it that proverbial moment of silence for the dead in combat as well as for the civilian dead? Is it a way of marking a tear or mutilation in the text that would be equivalent to the rape of women? The takeover of civilian life? Mutilation of the combative rooster? The appropriation of poetry and indeed all language? The loss of innocence? I find these possibilities highly suggestive for Bishop's deconstruction of the national World War II narrative.

If we think about this poem as a text framed within the speaker's "gun-metal blue" window, the blank space then becomes a space for the reader to project what is in the mind after the sight of the dead rooster and hens in the ash-heap. Given the image of the "ash-heap" and its allusion to the mythical rising phoenix as well as the war's convention of the soldier as crucified Christ, one anticipates some kind of commentary on resurrection and Christian brotherhood. But isn't it ironic to position the Christian cru-cifixion symbol over the dead rooster and hens in the grave? Bishop seems to pass such heavy judgment against them. Yet during the actual war all Western nations believed that Christ protected them and that their soldiers were Christ-figures.

Throughout the second section of "Roosters," Bishop interrogates the heroism of the Christian brotherhood war convention underwriting the national war narrative by focusing on Peter's betrayal of Christ signaled by the crowing of the cocks, or roosters. While she does not explicitly address Roosevelt's condemnation of Italy's betrayal of France in the poem, this historical context seems to haunt her explicit subject: brotherly denial and betrayal in the face of military pressure.

"St. Peter's sin" is his denial of his brotherhood with Christ before the Roman military in order to avoid punishment and death. The New Testa-ment's rhetorical justification of Peter's denial is the fact that it does save his life and allows him to become the first "pope" or "father" of early Chris-tianity. But Bishop points out that he does not experience the forgiveness and resurrection promised to Christians. She suggests in the poem that for "poor heart-sick" Peter these moments remain only "mights":

> those cock-a-doodles yet might bless,
> his dreadful rooster come to mean forgiveness (*CP* 38)

The later construction of a "bronze cock on a porphyry/pillar" does not mean that forgiveness and resurrection took place. This architectural com-memoration is the Roman papacy's propagandistic attempt to represent Peter's forgiveness for his betrayal in order to legitimize his Christian heroic positioning as "Prince of the Apostles," "to convince / all the assembly" that roosters do more than "deny." The "cock on the pillar" redirects Chris-tians away from the action of betrayal to the action of forgiveness and redemption.

But a monument cannot forgive Peter any more than it can raise dead soldiers from the grave. All Peter's tears cannot undo his denial of Christ. The heroic "bronze cock" monument cannot cover its origins in the brutal story of how one civilian denied his bond to another before the military authorities in order to escape death. Brotherhood cannot divorce itself from brotherly betrayal.

By questioning the historical foundation of the Christian brotherhood convention in the nation's war narrative, Bishop also draws attention to the Roman Catholic Church's use of the brotherhood convention in European conquest history through the crusades and colonialism. A papal bull, for instance, divided South America between Portugal and Spain. Christian men in the crusades were told to die for Christ.

Bishop also seems interested in the Roman Catholic Church's large role in colonialism and its accompanying human betrayals. Jesuits (brothers in the Society of Jesus) from many European backgrounds were major explorers in the western hemisphere: Marquette, for example, in North America. Their efforts were fueled in part by their zeal to transform their "heathen brethren" into "Christian brethren," for they were unable to see the Native Americans as true brothers until they were transformed into their Christian likeness.

Bishop inscribes the violent and militant Portuguese Christian colonization of Brazil in her poem "Brazil, January 1, 1502," written shortly after her arrival there in 1951. Here Christian soldiers sought the rape of Native American women. Because of the way that Bishop juxtaposes their attendance at Mass in the poem with the attempted "catch" or rape of the women, she suggests that the mass somehow legitimizes the soldiers' entitlement to their "catch."

In addition to the attempted rapes, the soldiers also were interested in capturing the women for the European slave market. By 1502 the Portuguese were heavily involved in the slave trade. As Hortense Spillers has pointed out, we learn from "Gomese Eannes de Azaurar's 'Chronicle of the Discovery and Conquest of Guinea 1441–1448' . . . that the Portuguese probably gain the dubious distinction of having introduced black Africans to the European market of servitude" (62). Roman Christianity thus has an uneasy relation to Western culture's system of violence and violation, which Pope John Paul II addressed on March 12, 2000 in his apology to the world ("Apology," *The New York Times,* A1, A10).

Given the religious bigotry of World War II's historical "moment," it is not surprising that Bishop raises the issue of religion within the Christian brotherhood convention of the nation's war narrative. The dominant reading of "Christian brotherhood" would have been "Protestant brotherhood" because the nation's long-held narrative of itself emphasized its heroic Puritan origins—and the Puritan flight from (Anglican) Anglo-Catholic domination and persecution.

In "Roosters," Bishop reveals that the "Protestant brotherhood" is not any more honorable than any other kind of brotherhood. First of all, it is linked to Rome historically because it originates with the Roman Catholic papacy and therefore shares a common historical bond with Catholicism. St. Peter, as the first pope and therefore founder of the Church, is inevitably linked to Roman Catholicism, and he is symbolically linked to the rooster, in a quite natural way, by the biblical denial tied to the crowing of the cock.

Unlike the national narrative with its interpretation of Christian as WASP, Bishop's poem reads Christian as early Roman Catholic. By doing this, she draws attention to the fact that all Christians were bonded as one in earlier history and that Protestantism represents a separation from the larger Christian brotherhood, or breech and betrayal, depending upon one's point of view. Moreover, Protestants were not free of the history of colonial conquest and expansion. Indeed, in North America alone they made their goal the complete domination of the continent and the subjugation and eradication of its indigenous peoples. Thus the very notion of "Protestant brotherhood" complicates the heroic notions of brotherly bonding of the national war narrative.

While the nation's war discourse spotlighted brotherhood and brotherly love, then, it had a very specific idea of who was to be included and excluded from brotherly embrace. In addition to a thorny history with Roman Catholics and the nation's indigenous peoples, the white Christian Protestant brotherhood—as well as the Roman Catholic community—ignored its "brotherly" responsibilities to the Jewish appeals to allow Jewish migration from Nazi domination. One of the most public anti-Semitic spokesman of the time was the Roman Catholic priest Charles E. Coughlin, known as "Father Coughlin." Bishop's spotlight on Peter's denial to the Roman officers draws attention to the era's anti-Semitism by emphasizing the origination of Roman Christianity in a Jewish historical "moment" of military subjugation and imperial colonialism. The Roman military was concerned with maintaining its hold over its Jewish subjects. The U.S. government denial of the Jewish refugees seems like a repetition of an earlier Christian denial in the face of military oppression. Jewish authorities of the time, we are told, colluded in Christ's crucifixion; but Peter was not in this "establishment." "Saint" Peter was instead the first Christian "father"—and he denied his Jewish brother Christ, who died at the hands of the Roman military dictatorship. Bishop's aim at the Roman papacy seems prescient from our perspective today as the debate over Pope Pius XII's silence during the war ensues.

Her targeting of the Roosevelt administration, since the president represented the heroic brotherhood of the nation, is also prescient from today's vantage point. As we now know, Roosevelt failed to override public anti-Semitism and to use immigration more heavily to save Jewish and other European refugee lives during the early years of the war. Estimates show that Roosevelt worked behind the scenes and allowed about 105,000 refugees to emigrate between 1933 and 1940 (Goodwin 101). But many opportunities were lost. When William Shulte of Indiana tried to broaden the visitor visas to any European child under sixteen, the bill was defeated in Congress because British boys and girls were Christian, and German children were mostly Jewish (Goodwin 101). So British children were welcomed, and the Germans were shut out for the most part. Refugee ships like the *St. Louis* that attempted to disembark in both Havana and Miami in 1939 were generally turned away, or only a handful of passengers were allowed to enter because they had the correct papers (Goodwin 101-2; 174-76).

In the poem, Bishop continues to challenge the legitimacy of the heroic male brotherhood convention by stating:

> St. Peter' sin
> was worse than that of Magdalen
> whose sin was of the flesh alone (*CP* 37)

This statement reverses conventional Catholic theology and with it centuries of Christian misogynistic representation of Magdalene's sin as the greatest sin, releasing "Magdalen" from the "captivity" of Christian brotherly/priestly discourse, which has depended upon her subjugation and denial.

Bishop's reference to "Magdalen" also draws attention to the Christian discourse that holds a binary "captive" vision of women as either Magdalene (to be destroyed) or Madonna (to be saved), which is related to military discourse as well. The "Magdalen" or prostitute is used to satisfy sexual desire but not procreation; thus she is expendable once her sexual services are completed because she does not serve the state's needs for soldiers, or human "ammunition." When the nation is culturally represented, the "Magdalen[s]" are ignored and the focus turns to women as Madonna figures, or mothers of the state. Yet women's positioning as mothers does not protect them in war, either, as the death of the "hens" in the first part of "Roosters" reveals. In either role, women are "captive" to male domination.

Following the refutation against the Christian male bonding conventions of militarism, the poem's speaker returns to the "broccoli" and the bedroom window—to the bloody-feathered mass grave of rooster and hens overlaid with the Christ-Peter-Magdalene imagery. The speaker wonders, "how could the night have come to grief?" Then the speaker watches the sun dawn on the scene, "following 'to see the end' / faithful as enemy, or friend," Bishop's reworking of the biblical story as Peter vowed to follow Christ to the end. This language is reminiscent of the language of aubade in the Great War battlefield where, as Fussell points out, the dawn revealed the deadly work of night in battle and/or the beginning of an enemy attack (51-64). He writes, "It was a cruel reversal that sunrise and sunset, established by over a century of Romantic poetry and painting as the tokens of hope and peace and rural charm, should now be exactly the moments of heightened ritual anxiety" (*The Great War & Modern Memory* 52).

Yet whereas the sun brought with it clarity in the death-haunted dawns of the Great War, the sun here brings only questions. While Peter resolved to covertly follow Christ to his end after his public betrayal, that was, as Lynn Keller suggests, little consolation (*Re-Making It New* 91). So why does Bishop end with this line that suggests that it is difficult to distinguish between enemy and friend?

Paradox here seems to place us again as readers on a battlefield in Great War soldiers' writings where, as Gilbert points out, the soldiers confront betrayal and rift in male comradeship as "not just accidental but essential consequences of war" (219). Emblematical of this kind of writing for Gilbert is Owen's poem "Strange Meeting," in which brotherly doubles meet and tell the other "I am the enemy you killed, my friend" (219). But Bishop's poem is not set in a World War I European battlefield—it takes place in civilian Key West, Florida.

Once again, Bishop draws the battlefield into the civilian world and confronts the reader in the poem's last line with unsettling concerns that previously may have faced only combatants: How does the culture of a military state affect human relationships? Human trust? How does one resolve the choice that the civilian Peter made between his own life and his loyalty to brotherhood when questioned by the Roman military? How does one live with it later? How does one live with it if this military state "moment" passes and another, more fortuitous government bringing peace emerges that would have made such a choice impossible to imagine? How does one choose the trustworthy if Christ himself was betrayed by his closest friend? Who is trustworthy in one context and not in another? To what extent did Peter have freedom of choice? To what extent is an individual subject subjugated to the ideology of his or her nation or military state? To what extent is the individual free within this ideology?

Most importantly, however, Bishop leaves the reader pondering the horrifying premise behind a military state that is implied in Peter's denial of Christ here: that one must deny the human bond with one's friend if she or he is designated as the enemy, the one to be arrested by the authorities. Even more appalling is the fact that one must deny one's general humanity and be prepared to kill the enemy or be killed by him or her or by one's own soldiers or military authorities for failure to kill or for treason. One must be prepared to kill a former friend if so ordered by the authorities because that friend is now named an enemy.

Bishop foresees the civilian reality as it is placed in the middle of warfare and the pastoral world of the barnyard becomes a battlefield. For her, war is not a marked space but can be anywhere—as World War II proved. Most importantly, however, Bishop points out that the war enters the mind, the imagination, dreaming, lovemaking, and the other most intimate parts of human living by drawing the scene of the roosters and the crucifixion into the bedroom of the speaker. Indeed, in the poem "Late Air," just two poems before "Songs for a Colored Singer" in the collection *North & South,* Bishop says that the red lights on the navy yard aerial are witnesses to nighttime love (*CP* 45).

No human space is exempt from the ravages of militarism. Civilians cannot escape it. Schweik persuasively argues: "Drawing the Peter/crucifixion analogy *inward*—into the bedroom, that sphere of the private, the domestic, the feminine, the sexual, the dream—it implicates the woman speaker in psychic structures of conflict, violence, and betrayal formerly reserved for specifically male or vaguely generalized others" (231-32).

As this book has discussed, Bishop has a very specific lesbian or bisexual context for considering the disruption of war—her own private love life. Consider, for instance, her letter indicating that she and Stevens felt compelled to flee the scene. Bishop enacts in the poem what war theorist Cynthia Enloe urged at a conference on women and war at Harvard in 1984: that we understand war as an ideological struggle rather than strictly as a physical or diplomatic event . . . and that we must move beyond the exceptional, marked event, which takes place on a militarized or public front, to include the private domain and the landscape of the mind (Higonnet 46). So while Bishop's concerns about anti-Semitism and "difference" in the poem are quasi-visible, her quasi-(in)visible, more personal anxieties about homophobia also inform it.

★   ★   ★

In addition to expressing her anti-Fascism as well as her general concerns about military governments and the U.S. wartime national narrative's constructions of nation, cultural production, war, gender, class, ethnicity, and race in "Roosters," Bishop also brought her war anxieties to her other major World War II poem, "Songs for a Colored Singer," published in 1944. Bishop said that it was for Billie Holiday, but very vaguely (*OA* 478). While the issue of race is highly visible in the songs just as it was in both the home front and war front cultures of the Second World War—"Colored" in the title was the accepted form from the NAACP used by both races—a hidden lesbian subtext also coexists.

The question of racism in "Songs" first surfaced in Adrienne Rich's comment that this "is a white woman's attempt—respectful, I believe—to speak through a Black woman's voice. A risky undertaking, and it betrays the failure and clumsiness of such a position" (35). The first two songs do indeed sound like Bishop's attempt to replicate the kind of song that she owned in her remarkable collection of private recordings by Holiday— except that, as Axelrod has correctly pointed out, Bishop's blues fail to acknowledge the centrality of white racism in the life of African Americans as most African American blues do ("Was Elizabeth Bishop a Racist?" 347; Fountain 75). But Bishop probably failed to understand this, for she was steeped in the stereotypes of African Americans that her dominant culture had perpetuated, just as she may not have understood completely why Brooks was embarrassed when Bishop said in her presence that as a child she had smeared burnt cork or coal on her own face and played in blackface (Fountain 315).

With the third song, Bishop shifts unexpectedly from imitating blues recordings that one would generally expect to hear in the public setting of a club, on the radio, or on a recording. We find ourselves reading a lullaby in the private setting of a bedroom. The image of Holiday at the microphone disappears, replaced by an adult with a child. Given the context of the title and the first two songs, however, it is difficult to imagine who else, besides Holiday or another blues singer, Bishop had in mind for the "adult" with the child.

Yet this doubling between an unspecified "adult" and an inferred female African American singer requires exploration. On one hand, the lullaby reads as a song of consolation about war. Travisano offers this kind of reading. He points out that the poem proposes that while war has wreaked havoc with reproduction and motherhood, the mother and child image in the wavelike rhythms of the poem prevails against the juxtaposed battleship, providing a kind of consolation (*Elizabeth Bishop* 86). Given Bishop's childhood experience in the Great War—her agonizing move to the United States and her ill mother's injury in the collision of ships in Halifax—the song can be read as a poignant consolation to herself and other children in war.

Because the song is set in a room that seems to be a kind of bedroom or nursery space, one is reminded of the bedroom window in "Roosters" and the scenes of battle outside of it:

> Lullaby.
> Adult and child
> Sink to their rest.
> At sea the big ship sinks and dies,
> lead in its breast. (*CP* 49)

In the next two stanzas, the lullaby's singer juxtaposes the war and childhood:

> Let nations rage,
> let nations fall.
> The shadow of the crib makes an enormous cage
> upon the wall.
>
> Sleep on and on,
> war's over soon.
> Drop the silly, harmless toy,
> pick up the moon. (*CP* 49)

In the fourth stanza, the singer tells the child not to pay attention to those who might say "you have no sense" because "it won't make no difference." The final stanza repeats the first.

When this "lullaby" is read intertextually against the national narrative of the "democratic family" in which the family functions as a kind of school for democracy, however, its complexity begins to emerge. The universal adult and child imagery is inclusive across social boundaries; the African American female adult and child reminds one that the society is segregated and unequal in its treatment of its citizens.

Whether one reads the juxtaposition of adult and child (or African American female and child) against the sunken ship as comforting or disquieting, the fact that the poem is a "lullaby" is significant. Lullabies are songs for lulling children to sleep. While the adult lullaby singer attempts to soothe over anxieties about war, she (or he) also is teaching about war. This socializes the child into what Julia Kristéva has called the violent structures of culture, for which one is rewarded (116). The innocent childhood song form of the lullaby, then, is intertwined here with cultural systems of violence and war.

The incongruity between "adult and child" in the text and the implied African American woman and child draws attention to both men and women, for both comprise the U.S. citizenry, and thereby rewrites the home front convention of mother/child as adult/child. Bishop effectively challenges the reader's automatic assumption that the image is one of mother and child simply because this is the image of the dominant discourse. She also revises the assumption inherent in such thinking as Kristéva's that mothers automatically are the ones to socialize children into violence. Moreover, she revises the reliance of cultural conventions of war on the *pièta* imagery of sorrowing mother over dying soldier-son and draws attention to the fact that adults—and not only mothers—give their children to the state's military order.

Finally, she intimates that war deprives children of maternal love and protection. In the horrifying realities of war, mothers are brutalized, injured, and killed and may not be able to parent their own children. This happened to Bishop. U.S. anxieties about this were quite high in the World War II era. One of the most famous photos in the war during the 1937 Japanese aggression in China depicted an "abandoned Chinese child, injured, bleeding, bawling on its haunches" in the burning Shanghai railway station (Engelhardt 239). The popular "horror of war" bubble-gum series announced, "War Against Women & Children/ Don't Let It Happen Over Here!" (Engelhardt 239).

Bishop unsettles conventional expectations in the lullaby even further by juxtaposing the adult/child dyad against the battleship but not specifying whether the ship is "enemy" or "friendly" and thereby raising the earlier question in the conclusion to "Roosters": how does one differentiate between enemy and friend? According to U.S. dominant rhetoric, the adult/child dyad would indicate the United States because the enemies' civilians were omitted in propaganda. Gubar writes persuasively:

> In popular magazines and newspapers, American and English photographs
> during the war depicted women and children as the predominant civilian
> casualties of blitzes, . . . pictures of Allied planes dropping bombs over both
> the Asian and European fronts tended to represent the transcendent Allied
> power without regard to the victims. (231)

Bishop works against this "omission" in her discourse. The ship sinks to its rest with lead in its breast. When one considers that the ship is carrying dead men within it, one imagines a mother/child or parent/child dyad representing not only this death scene but also the civilian widows and orphans left behind as additional casualties of war. Thus the lesson that military attacks are automatically heroic and without civilian victims is undermined. Because the question of enemy or friend is left unresolved, the focus is on both enemy and friendly civilian victims.

This strategy of indeterminant imagery destabilizes not only gender and military conventions but also social class conventions. For example, if one considers the "adult" in the dyad to be a feminine figure, how does one go about identifying it further? One can just as easily decide that the figure is a wet nurse or a maid as well as the mother, or Holiday. Indeed, the stereotype of the "mammy" would have been reinforced if Bishop had written "mother and child."

Beyond destabilizing the dominant courtly love conventions in terms of social class (elitist/working), gender (male/female), and military (enemy/friend) hierarchies, Bishop also unsettles it in terms of race (black/white) binaries, beginning with the poem's title. As we have been discussing, the era's hegemonic national narrative generally centered on a white mother/child dyad. During World War II, the United States was predominantly racially segregated, and African Americans were segregated and treated unequally in the military. African Americans (and members of other ethnic groups) generally were given behind-the-lines noncombat service duties. Singers like Holiday sang in racially segregated clubs so nearly all of their audiences were white.

We clearly have a black singer designated here in the poem's title. Is she (or he) singing a lullaby to a white child or black child? To a representative child who encompasses both whites and blacks? To a white/black/representative adult or nation? Race does make a difference. If the child is a white male, then he is "ammunition" for war; if a white female, then she is the "bearer" of such "ammunition." If the child is an African-American male or female, then he or she is not central to U.S. militarism in this era either as a soldier or as a reason to save the nation from the enemy. In other words, the African American male or female is secondary in the militarist discourses of the soldier-savior and nation of "saved" faithful women and children. It is difficult to determine where such children are mapped if they are neither "in" nor "out" of the nation, obviously "present" but "unseen" within it.

Bishop's concerns about these issues likely stemmed from her concerns for the lives of civilians under military rule; and this would have included the African Americans she knew, like Holiday. The lullaby singer's indication that somehow the war and the nations raging at each other will make "no difference" to this child reveals that no matter who wins, this child's life will remain unaffected, for better or worse. The white he/she is already a captive subject to the nation who must give up life or give up child if the state goes to war. The African American he/she is a captive subject within the nation whose life was continually controlled by U.S. militarism. He/she was told "how to live" first in slavery, and then in "free" civilian life. Both legal and social codes governed everything from where to sit on buses and where to go to school to where to eat, where to drink, where to sleep, and so on.

More directly related to the stakes in World War II, African Americans found themselves fighting Fascist racism abroad and at home simultaneously. Nazism was intent on destroying massive numbers of peoples in a variety of minority groups. African Americans realized that they were one of these targeted groups. As Schweik points out persuasively, African American rhetoric in this war culture sometimes negotiated the racial struggle by juxtaposing domestic racial tensions against the more publicly recognized war atrocities. During 1942, for example, the slogan "remember Pearl Harbor and Sikeston too" appeared everywhere in the African American press as writers pointed to racism as both a foreign and domestic battle (Cleo Wright had been lynched at Sikeston, Missouri; see Schweik 320-24). Given this rhetorical context, it is instructive to consider the fact that Bishop may be attempting in her lullaby to explore racism.

The fourth song moves further into the bedroom—into the world of dream and focuses explicitly on images of Africanness, concluding with the image of an army of black faces. If Holiday is again intended as the singer, then the army's emergence signals eventual triumph. But again incongruity exists. If the poet is the speaker, then the poem's conclusion seems threatening, as Axelrod suggests ("Was Elizabeth Bishop a Racist?" 347-348). This song's confounding ending resembles the tenth stanza of "Faustina, or Rock Roses," in which the scene is either one of freedom or nightmare, or both. Moreover, if one considers this song in terms of the home front, an army seems hidden beneath the land—as in the photos of the war factory in California discussed earlier.

Yet the haunting black faces emerging from the leaves also remind us of suffering and death as the shining of the leaves is transformed into a tearful black face that multiplies into an "army." With Bishop's use of such evocative words as "curious flower or fruit," "black seeds" and "conspiring root,"

the song also seems to be Bishop's homage to Holiday's renowned performance of the protest song against lynching, the dirge "Strange Fruit." Holiday first sang the song in 1939 at the integrated Greenwich Village cabaret
Café Society, frequented by intellectuals, artists, and political leftists. Given
Louise Crane's pursuit of Holiday beginning in 1939, it is difficult to imagine that Bishop would not have known about the song, which generated a
momentous response when Holiday's recording of it for Commodore
Records was released in the summer of 1939 (see Margolick). Holiday's
voice instilled inescapable and unbearable horror in the listeners as she
phrased the haunting juxtaposition of a black body with "bulging eyes,
twisted mouth, and burning flesh swinging, strange fruit, from the poplar
trees" while magnolias sweeten and freshen the air.

While Bishop draws upon Holiday's "Strange Fruit," this song was not
her introduction to lynching and other racial violence. As a resident of
racially-segregated Florida, she could hardly have escaped such news. During the 1930s, the Ku Klux Klan had reasserted itself with night raids.
Twenty-eight known lynchings took place in 1933; eighty-three between
1933 and 1937. Historian Blanche Wiesen Cook states that "lynchings
were not merely public hangings, they were community ceremonies witnessed by mobs of men, women, and children who worked themselves into
bloodlust as torture and burning proceeded" and continued because campaigns to pass a federal anti-lynching law failed (*Eleanor Roosevelt*, v. 2, 177,
442).

Cook goes on to report the October 26, 1934, lynching in Alabama of
Claude Neal, accused of the murder of a white woman in Florida. Men,
women, and children cheered as he was tortured to death. She states, "After
an orgy of unspeakable violence and mutilation, the charred, disfigured
remains of a man hung from a tree in the courthouse square, and photographs were sold for fifty cents each" (243). Shortly afterwards, in February 1935, the NAACP mounted "Art Commentary on Lynching" in a
New York gallery, which included Reginald Marsh's award-winning *New
Yorker* illustration of a mother holding her child on her shoulders to get a
better view with the caption "This is her first lynching" (244). The frenzy
over lynching extended to northern urban areas as well. As Cook points
out, a Harlem mob of women on March 19, 1935, demanded that a young
boy caught stealing a ten cent penknife be beaten and lynched just as in the
South (256).

The lynching frenzy in the United States reflected the nation's racist
attitudes but also was linked to Fascist violence. As Cook states, "fascist bru-
tality and racialist rhetoric in Europe encouraged American lynchers.

America's failure to demonstrate official opposition encouraged racialist violence in Europe. The message seemed to be: Lynching was done, torture was acceptable" (246).

Violence in 1937, for example, the year that Congress might have passed a federal antilynching law, was occurring not only in lynchings in the United States but also in the Japanese invasion of China, the European Holocaust, and the Spanish Civil War. Bishop seemed to be quite attentive to European Fascism that year, offering the lost poem "War in Ethiopia" and her translation skills for poetry about the Spanish Civil War. But she did more than this.

"The Hanging of the Mouse" is dated 1937 and seems to address both European violence and American lynching. With its setting at the gallows in a town square, the brown beetle military escort of the criminal mouse, and the death sentence read by the king's messenger, readers sense that they are in a European world. However, the hanging's depiction as a public ceremonial event with large crowds assembling during the night with a feeling of celebration and sniffing with pleasure at the mouse's terror also ties it to American lynching.

Moreover, Bishop's inclusion of a mother cat who brought her kitten in her mouth recalls Marsh's illustration with the mother who put her child on her shoulders to see her first lynching. When the kitten squirms and shrieks as the mother's tears roll down its back, the mother cat thinks the hanging had been too distressing, but an "excellent moral lesson, nevertheless" (*CP* 145). Even more chilling in its implication of the induction of children into racial violence is Bishop's decision to have the hangman's young son spring the trap to kill the mouse.

Finally, Bishop attacks both military government and Christianity. The adult raccoon-executioner is depicted as a Pontius Pilate figure washing his hands of guilt. The praying (one think immediately also of preying) mantis is an incompetent character who despises being with the lowly and would rather not be there; but he performs his ministerial role nonetheless—in a bungling fashion.

Beneath this attempt to reach across racial boundaries is a quasi-(in)visible lesbian subtext that requires a knowledge of both Holiday's and Bishop's biographies. As mentioned earlier, Crane left Bishop in Key West in 1938 after their first few months together to pursue a lively life in the music scene of New York with occasional visits to their home together. Crane soon became infatuated with Holiday and the art world and gradually returned to Key West less and less often. Mary Meigs, a friend of both Bishop and Crane, said that Crane was passionately interested in Holiday:

"She told me she had followed Billie Holiday from night spot to night spot, while Billie, who refers to Louise in her autobiography as a 'rich white chick' was mistrustful" (Fountain 86).

Bishop did not handle the breakup easily. Crane told Meigs that she was filled with despair and threatened suicide (Fountain 86). After she made several trips to New York to try to recover the relationship with Crane, she finally gave up in July 1941, rented out the house, and moved in with Marjorie Stevens.

Bishop's poem "Letter to N.Y.," which is "for Louise Crane," appears in the volume *A Cold Spring* with poems that tend to post-date her Key West years. However, it depicts Crane's World War II–era lifestyle while Bishop was still pursuing her (*CP* 80). In the poem, the speaker teases Crane about telling her in her next letter about her life—the plays, but also the "pleasures" she pursues after the plays. She then imagines Crane taking cabs in the middle of the night and sitting in clubs filled with jokes and loud music until the sun almost rises. In the conclusion she presses Crane again to tell her what she is doing and where she is going.

So Bishop the poet had Holiday the singer as a rival for Crane's affections. But Bishop also developed a friendship with Holiday as well. She was very proud of her collection of private recordings that Holiday had made, although it is not clear if they were made for Crane and given to Bishop or if they were made for Bishop as well (Fountain 75). Joseph Summers recalls that Bishop liked Holiday and "loved her songs." She was proud of bringing Holiday and Ralph Kirkpatrick together to sing and play at her place (Fountain 104).

Many have admired and respected Holiday's singing style and paid tribute to her—Frank O'Hara, for example, in "The Day Lady Died."[4] But what specifically drew Bishop to her vocalization? One wonders if it was not Bishop's recognition that Holiday had mastered the ability to move easily between private disclosure and public announcement, the shared and the secret in her singing, exactly what Bishop was attempting to do in her own poetry (Pareles, Strauss, Ratliff, and Powers, B5).

Yet there is not the slightest hint of any relationship between the two women in the text of "Songs for a Colored Singer." Bishop could have been merely a fan. Hidden here in the poem, then, is the self-censorship of a common bond between the two women based on suppressed sexual affiliation in a nation struggling with homophobia. Indeed, their shared bond made them targets of Nazism, which had been punishing homosexuality brutally.[5] In addition, the hidden tie also reveals Bishop's awareness of racism among her readers and the culture at large.

"Songs for a Colored Singer" reveals, then, more provocative entanglements than one might expect, especially given the "version" of Bishop as silent following "Roosters." Clearly Bishop's anxieties about Nazism and American racial violence did not abate, nor did her concerns about the prospect of a U.S. military state, whether because of Nazi domination or the dominance of the Pentagon in national politics. By retrieving her concerns with such social constructions as nation, race, class, gender, cultural production, ethnicity, and sexual orientation, we are able to learn where Bishop succeeded and where she fell short in her attempts to write about the era.

Bishop faced even stronger challenges as the nation moved into the postwar and early Cold War years. The next chapter takes up her conflicted positioning with war and militarization in the emerging midcentury victory culture, beginning with her unread poetry fragment "V–Day August 14th, 1945."

Chapter 5 ↶

WATCHING THE COLD WAR BEGIN

On V-Day in 1945, Bishop saw a tattered world from her window-sill as she looked out at the torn streamers from the nation's victory celebrations and ticker-tape parades. A barely decipherable handwritten poetry fragment entitled "V-Day August 14th, 1945" in the Vassar College archives that has gone unnoted reveals Bishop's anxieties about the war and foreshadows her difficulties in negotiating a Cold War narrative intent on the militarization of domestic and foreign policy.

When the war ended and the U.S. military returned, thousands cheered with paper streamers in ticker-tape parades like the widely photographed New York City parade. Bishop was not one of them. She wrote about the way that the streamers reminded her of a flock of birds pinned down in a siege (Folder 75.3a, p. 73, VC). Instead of simply evoking the parade streamers of the "victorious" and "saved" national hegemonic war narrative in which women and families greeted the honorable returning U.S. soldiers, Bishop's imagery carries multilayered connotations. It recalls imagery evoked from an earlier window sill at "the gun-metal blue window"—in "Roosters" with its birds (or fliers and planes) who are seen as doomed—only now fragmented language replaces the more traditional narrative poetic flow:

> and one is flying,
> with raging heroism defying
> even the sensation of dying.
>
> And one has fallen . . .
> his torn-out, bloodied feathers drift down. (*CP* 37)

The image of playing children in "V-Day August 14th, 1945" also recalls both the complexity of the child's voice in "Roosters" and the violated intimate world of innocence in the lullaby for Holiday and "The Hanging of the Mouse."

The poem evokes no celebration. There is no trace of the "official story" already being crafted about the atomic bombs that ended the war and ushered in the Cold War: namely, that the "bomb" was the savior of both American and Japanese lives, a contested story within U.S. culture that originated shortly after the war and that continues today (Hein 29). For example, George Kennan, usually associated with "containment" because he introduced the term in an early postwar policy statement, believed by the early 1950s that the use of the atomic bomb against the Japanese was "regrettable extremism" (Engelhardt 112).[1]

Indeed, Bishop's poetry fragment can be read as a devastating and controversial double text for two apparently oppositional large-scale events in the year 1945: the bombing of the Axis enemy, Japan, which ended the war, as well as the public revelation of the Holocaust victimization by Nazi Germany that was part of their war atrocities. In the reading of Japan, the tattered streamers, for example, remind one of the remnants of civilian human skin and clothing reported at Hiroshima and Nagasaki following the atomic bombings upon which this new Cold War dominant victory narrative was won and mapped. Masako Taorezu has said that the "bodies" in the bombings were "like peeled peaches" (Braw 165). In the reading of the Holocaust, the torn pieces of paper recall the treatment of Jews and other identified enemies of the Third Reich as body parts, commodities to support and finance Nazi goals. For example, gold was extracted from teeth, sperm used for genetic experimentation, and blood collected for so-called scientific research.

While nowhere in her writing does Bishop reveal that she is aware of this double text, historical context for this interpretation exists in Engelhardt's *The End of Victory Culture.* In his discussion of the end of the war, he points out that only a few critics like Lewis Mumford and Dwight Macdonald made a link between "the two great industrial processes of death that emerged from twentieth-century war" (58). In her juxtaposition of the horrific images of destruction against the depiction of children at play, Bishop draws attention to a large-scale loss of innocence. Certainly this describes the result of the initial public revelation of the vast dimension of the Holocaust, a dimension that continues to grow in scale today with such news as unresolved confiscated Jewish funds in European banks, abuse of insurance policies of Jewish camp victims, forced Jewish labor in profitable German factories, and stolen art treasures in galleries and museums around the world.

The poem also portrays the response of some Americans as they realized that the atomic bombing had ushered in an unknown future filled with the dangers of nuclear tragedy. As Engelhardt writes, the "great fear" that "we," not "they," might be the next victims of nuclear extermination was to chase Americans through the coming decades" (56). Almost immediately after the bombing, the media began to speculate on the nation's vaporization (Engelhardt 56-57).

This national ceremony of V-Day in the form of a victory peace parade thus is intertwined with the war's system of violence against civilians in Bishop's poetry fragment. This reveals her skepticism about the emerging Cold War military culture of "containment" that promised to build world peace from the "torn bits" or "pieces" of civilians. World War II had originated in the Axis's deliberate attempted erasure of the human subjectivity of thousands of Jews, Chinese, and other targeted groups, for, as Scarry points out, pieces of human bodies fragmented by weapons carry only the marks of military power and no sense of person (267). Many in the United States had recoiled at the Holocaust and German war atrocities as well as the Japanese aggression against China and other war crimes, including the systematic killing of 300,000 Chinese civilians and prisoners in Nanking, a city with fewer than 650,000 people in 1937. Many also questioned the Allied bombings of German cities; and at the end of the war the atomic bombing of Japan incited controversy about new kinds of warfare and the responsible, ethical resolution of conflict.

When Bishop witnessed the "peace," she offered only the barest kind of "piece," with disconnected phrases and imagery, as though a fall into silence was the most appropriate response. This stripped-down, reader-resistant, quasi-(in)visible rhetoric contrasted sharply with the public bravado of some of the emerging Cold War dominant discourse. Indeed, in relation to Bishop's own fully fleshed-out poem "Roosters," this fragment offers a kind of linguistic and visual depiction of a world and language left in tatters.

For her, the message of the torn parade streamers was not peace, but the prospect of more escalating horrific warfare and global military government. In her anxieties she was not alone. Other poets, including Jarrell and Lowell, were writing about the atomic bombing. By 1950 a conclave of leading clergymen in the federal Dun Commission issued the statement: "War is the culture of our age and the culture is war" (Boyer 348).

★ ★ ★

With the close of the war, U.S. national government leaders focused on changing the war plot from World War II to Cold War "containment" with the intent of remapping the globe into a bipolar world of Communism and Free West. (Both sides intended to become the leader of the entire globe eventually.) The Soviet Union as well as Communist China and the United States saw themselves as the salvific leaders of each sphere and locked into geopolitical struggle. What did Bishop—and the nation—see as this new U.S. military discourse emerged with its revision of the World War II courtly love/captivity and male-bonding conventions?

To answer this question, one must remember that several Cold War national narratives existed in the beginning, just like the situation in the Second World War. Roosevelt's interventionist narrative came to dominate World War II–era culture only gradually, with many kinds of competing pacifist, antimilitarist, and right-wing isolationist narratives in the political marketplace before its hegemony and, to a lesser extent, afterwards. In the immediate postwar period, President Harry Truman as well as Kennan tried to form a new U.S. foreign policy to address anxieties about Communism that relied heavily on new diplomatic goals.[2] The political right led by Joseph McCarthy, Richard Nixon, and J. Edgar Hoover, however, focused on building up a military-driven domestic and foreign policy as well as public hysteria to fuel its decisions. Katharine Graham, whose paper was attacked by McCarthy's right wing for its liberalism, remembers that "there were . . . genuine, strong reasons for anticommunism. . . . Abroad . . . in 1948 the communists took over in Czechoslovakia. Obviously, there were real concerns, but the political exploitation and misuse of them was shameless. . . . The political right kept manipulating America's fears in a demagogic way, and the atmosphere grew more poisonous as the Cold War grew more intense" (193).

Nadel offers a useful description in *Containment Culture* of U.S. "containment" culture that seems quite relevant here. He describes it as a gendered heterosexual courtship romance plot like the one we have been discussing. This time, however, the "beloved" white middle or upper-class female "hunted" United States must be saved from the demonic male hunter Communism instead of Germany, Italy, and Japan. His paradigm accurately reflects Kennan's intentions in his 1948 essay, "The Sources of Soviet Conduct," when he first broached the term "containment" in relationship to the Soviet Union in the emerging new U.S. foreign policy (4). (Kennan later renounced "containment" as unworkable.)

As in World War II's victory plot, a "double plot" depicted both the enemy as well as U.S. civilians or citizens. The new war discourse closely resembled the World War II version, in which U.S. soldiers had sought to rescue the faithful feminine U.S. nation from the clutches of demonic Nazis, Fascists, and Japanese and to "master" or "contain" or "destroy" the feminine-coded enemy—be it primarily male combatants or predominantly female civilians. As a result, the "containment" narrative focused on changing the enemy's face first.

The transformation of the enemy's face occurred gradually during the late 1940s in the mass media and popular culture. The nation's government felt betrayed by the Soviet Communists in treaty negotiations on their maneuvering in Germany and their takeover of Eastern Europe following the war. The betrayal was cast in rhetoric similar to the language used when Italy "betrayed" France to Nazi Germany. An essay in 1946 entitled "Red Fascism Confronts Religious America" in *Catholic World,* for example, noted that only color separated "Red Fascism" from "Brown Fascism" (Ginder 491).

But Communism was not seen merely as an enemy limited to the Soviet-held geopolitical empire, to be fought primarily on foreign soil in order to prevent attacks on the United States, as had been the case in World War II. The United States was seen as vulnerable from within the nation. So the nation's "containment" courtship plot also was a "double plot." The goal was to rescue the feminized nation from Communist subversion and treason but also to dictate, police, and penetrate the civilian or private citizen realm—exactly what Bishop had deplored so much in the Second World War.

Rhetoric characterizing the nation's need to "contain" Communism can be found in the discourses of such early right-wing ardent "containment" anti-Communist leaders as Hoover and Nixon. This discursive strategy continued unabated for a long time in the language of Hoover and Nixon, as revealed, for example, in their later statements for the documentary *Seeing Red: Stories of American Communists.* Hoover stated in the film:

> It is a way of life—an evil and malignant way of life. It reveals a condition akin to disease that spreads like an epidemic. And like an epidemic a quarantine is necessary to keep it from infecting this nation. (1)

Nixon warned:

> I've . . . heard some people say, 'After all, they're a bunch of rats, why don't we go out and shoot them?' Well, I agree that the Communists are rats. (14)

Popular culture also depicted domestic Communists as dangerous. Comic books, for example, cast cowboy heroes like Roy Rogers against them. In one plot line, Rogers stopped a Communist attempt to spread the aftosa virus among western cattle ranches that used a traveling medicine show peddling bottles of infected horse liniment. Rogers's response to the sheriff's query about who would want to destroy America's beef supply was that the United States has enemies who "hate everything American!" The comic-book industry had experimented fitfully with new storylines based on the Third Reich—one comic book conjectured that Hitler had moved to an underground city beneath Yellowstone National Park to plan his next rise to power—and then settled upon the "Red Menace" with its full energy (Savage 71).

The final twist in the demonism of the enemy was its feminization. World War II discourse had equated the enemy with dangerous, deadly, and diseased "femme fatale" women who were actually disguised spies and informants, and so Cold War discourse cast Communism in dreaded sexual and maternal imagery. Nixon, Hoover, and the comic-book industry drew upon this kind of war discourse in their focus on disease and poisoning. They expected their audiences to fill in the feminized discourse they left blank because World War II discourse was so fresh in their minds. An advertisement from the nation's Electric Light and Power Companies, for example, in the May 22, 1950, issue of *Time* used the code word "socialistic" for "Communist" and cast its "allure" in terms of the painting *Odysseus and the Sirens*. The advertisement warned the reader against the sirens' "soothing song" of "socialism," cautioning against the governmental control of business and announcing "the threat of a socialistic America is everyone's problem—because it is everyone's danger!" (Electric Light & Power Council 6).

The male role in this courtship model was very rigidly defined along conventional gender expectations and focused sharply on Communism as the enemy. American men were dispatched to protect the U.S. nation—personified through its land and business enterprises as well as women—on both foreign and domestic soil. But this time their role had moved exclusively from the physical battlefront. The nation's returning soldier was to find, in the words of a Greyhound bus advertisement, "Journey's Beginning," from the era, "secure congenial post-war employment, to renew friendships with his wartime buddies, to enjoy the Land he fought for . . ." in the same issue of *Time* as the power company ad (8).

As the welcoming nation figures of the mother and younger sister indicate in this ad, white women were placed in supportive roles to the returning men in the nation's Cold War courtly love plot. I deliberately use the words "were placed" here because so many women had entered the workplace during World War II; and not all were eager to return to the home. Collaboration between U.S. magazines and the national government directed women into their conventional gender roles again at the end of war, as such studies as Maureen Honey's *Creating Rosie the Riveter* document (40). The nation's women were given the task of mothering a new generation in U.S. democracy. While the men were expected to assume leadership as civilian-soldiers, the women were expected to address the physical needs of the home and family, not only by procreating but by becoming consumers to supply the "nuclear family." Procreation, as Elaine May and Stephanie Coontz have demonstrated, was regarded as a civic virtue and fell heavily upon the women.

Given, however, the woman's contradictory negative/positive role in the national "containment" courtly love convention, it is difficult to ignore the way that the double rhetorics of procreation and disease illustrate militarist discourse's evasion of the requirements of rational discourse. Why ask the diseased or afflicted feminine to procreate if one is interested in a more purified nation-state? The incredulous answer to this reveals the dangerous machinations of a military state. Cold War militarists and the political right used their definition of "her disease" to justify policing and "purification" or purging.

Advertisers barraged the U.S. public with the message that the home front was simultaneously a warfront extending from World War II. A Mack truck advertisement in *Time* on April 24, 1950, for example, featured a Mack truck that had been transformed from an army truck. The visuals are reinforced by the headline "From war to peace." But underneath this message is another, more important one: that the peacetime Mack truck was also still a war-related truck to be employed in the new consumer Cold War—and ready for actual warfront use at any time (9). As Stephen J. Whitfield writes, "what enhanced the home was not unrelated to what protected the homeland" (74). The companies that produced large consumer products like kitchen appliances were also major weapons contractors (Engelhardt 78).

Whereas a good patriotic white American civilian during World War II was defined as a home front or battlefront supporter of the Allies—or at least a silent skeptic—the focus in Cold War "containment" shifted the issue of patriotism and good citizenship more fully to the private sphere of the family and home. This new right-wing military culture penetrated the U.S. civilian world in order to transform it into another field for "social control" so that it could wage a consumer war against Communism. As Nadel points out, the potential for domestication differentiated between

"American" and "un-American" activity; and those outside of the nuclear family framework (for example, homosexuals; single, divorced, and widowed men and women; orphans; displaced persons and refugees) were said to manifest behavior that challenged the social—that is, military—order (121, 124). The definition of patriotism was clearly "domestication."

This Cold War national narrative's resemblance to Fascist Germany's narrative was seen immediately by many, especially when Nixon, Hoover, McCarthy, and the House on Un-American Activities Committee (HUAC) stepped into the national discourse. As indicated, Nixon and Hoover depicted Communism in terms of both disease and women, suggesting that only the nation's men could restore the nation to its idealized glory. The rhetoric sounds Fascist, with the Communists replacing the Jews, intellectuals, and other subversives. Women were seen for their value as procreators of the nation's military; men were to be soldiers; children were to assume civilian policing duties, monitoring neighbors for Communist activity. Civilian spying was encouraged, sanctioned, and rewarded—a problematical move when one considers the U.S. representation of itself as a democracy.

Newspaper political cartoonist Herblock saw the grave implications very early. Graham recounts his work in the *Post*'s acrimonious struggle with McCarthy and HUAC as "searing and powerful." The May 16, 1948, political cartoon, for example, depicted Nixon and two others, "all dressed as Puritans . . . building a fire under a chained Statue of Liberty and saying: 'We've got to burn the evil spirits out of her'" (203). While the welcoming faithful nation—represented in the statue of liberty—to which the "victorious" World War II soldiers had returned was seen by some leaders like Nixon as diseased by Communism, Herblock suggests that these same leaders may bring their own disease and danger to the nation and destroy it.

Another text here seems equally repressive, for it also appears that these same leaders think of the feminized nation as having been seduced in their absence—perhaps by their temporary roles in the male world of the workplace. The "feminized" nation had to be "chained" or "contained" for its "treatment or cure," obviously having consorted with the "enemy" and betrayed the soldiers in their absence. Transgression of gender spaces could not be tolerated.

The right-wing takeover of the private sphere of U.S. life extended to cultural production as well. It exploited mercilessly a September 24, 1946, letter "American Relations with the Soviet Union," in which Kennan advocated using cultural "intoxication." He urged that to the "greatest extent tolerated by the Soviet Government, we should distribute books, magazines and movies among the Soviets, beam radio broadcasts to the U.S.S.R., and press for an exchange of tourists, students, and educators" (Gaddis 68).

Kennan's proposal about the use of culture soon became national policy, as President Dwight Eisenhower indicated later in a San Francisco speech of October 8, 1952:

> Our aim in "Cold War" is not conquest of territory or subjugation by force. Our aim is more subtle, more pervasive, more complete. We are trying to get the world, by peaceful means, to believe the truth. . . . The means we shall employ to spread this truth are often called "psychological.". . . Psychological warfare is the struggle for the minds and will of men. (Cook, *The Declassified Eisenhower* 121)

Cultural production and producers were pressed to serve the nation in the attainment of two interrelated goals: the eradication of the Communist disease within the nation's "house" and the creation of a cultural rhetoric for the international Cold War front resembling the propaganda used in the Second World War. The U.S. political right felt it had sufficient justification to appropriate, read, and govern cultural production because of security interests, as its well-known foray into Hollywood "blacklisting" amply demonstrates.

While debate existed over how to respond to the Soviet Union and "Red" China, intellectual liberals gradually signaled their move into a mainstream consensus. Arthur Schlesinger, Jr.'s *The Vital Center,* for example, advocated an anticommunist stance with an emphasis on the value of human liberties, thereby creating a private sphere hegemonic discourse that agreed with the nation's official narrative of "anticommunism." As long as one could prove one's "anticommunism" credentials, one had a certain degree of freedom for differing or at least not being as propagandistically "celebrative."

Writers were not forced into one viewpoint, although the "moment" demanded extreme caution. By 1952, both *The Nation* and *Partisan Review* felt compelled to publish special issues articulating the new role of intellectuals and artists. Carey McWilliams at *The Nation* focused on "How Free is Free?" as the issue asked difficult questions about McCarthyism and intellectual repression and dissent, and propounded a guarded view of the United States. The *Partisan Review,* a widely respected publication of the anti-Stalinist left in the 1930s, sponsored a colloquium on "Our Country and Our Culture" over the space of three issues that advocated a surprising move, which tells us a great deal about the pressure that 1930s socialists, Communists, and leftists felt in their effort to escape HUAC scrutiny. It argued for an affirmative and celebratory vision of the new Cold War or postwar United States. The editors announced that "America has become the protector of Western civilization. . . . The cultural consequences are bound to be far-reaching. . . . For better or worse, most writers no longer accept alienation as the artist's fate in America; on the contrary, they want very much to be part of American life" (284). James Burnham argued: "The objective justification for the intellectuals' 'reaffirmation and redis- covery of America' is . . . political and military. . . . A world political or military victory of the Soviet totalitarianism is the worst possible secular evil" (290).

Within the Cold War victory narrative, cultural producers and intellec- tuals were conscripted into the international Cold War to be "ambassadors" of the United States and preservers of European culture and history to support the nation's new role as the major "Western" power responsible for the Western past and future. In other words, they were expected to embrace fully the new and enlarging domestic sphere of the nation as it took in Europe and other "client" nations under its military protection and "Americanized" these annexes with U.S. culture, consumer goods, and mil- itarism. Cultural production was thus domesticated and feminized and appropriated for military use, whether the producer consented or not. Not surprisingly, poets found themselves pressed to engage, according to von Hallberg, in nation-building "accomodationist" poetry (95).

But even the intellectuals and writers who sought "containment" within the emerging Cold War cultural narrative saw problems for themselves. Newton Arvin wrote that "the artist and intellectual who wants to be a part of American life is faced with a mass culture which makes him feel that he is still outside looking in. . . . America is a nation where at the same time cultural freedom is promised and mass culture produced" (284-85).

In such an artistic "moment," what were the expectations for men and women writers? In World War II discourse, the men held the privileged position of the front-liner or soldier-poet. In "containment" culture, they were expected to follow their nation's lead. Indeed most of the participants of the "Our Country and Our Culture" symposium were men, including James Agee, Jacques Barzun, Saul Bellow, R. P. Blackmur, Richard Chase, Ralph Ellison, Leslie Fiedler, Sidney Hook, Irving Howe, Alfred Kazin, C. Wright Mills, Reinhold Niebuhr, Philip Rahv, John Crowe Ransom, David Reisman, Delmore Schwartz, Arthur Schlesinger, Jr., Allen Tate, Lionel Trilling, Robert Penn Warren, and Richard Wilbur. Norman Mailer participated but was the only writer who also dissented. The "mainstreaming" of the artist was a strong enough imperative to prompt Jarrell to decry the arrival of the poet in the "gray flannel suit," like that of the protagonist in Sloan Wilson's bestselling 1950s novel *The Man in the Gray Flannel Suit* (September 5, 1956, Folder 5.8, VC). Jarrell's uncanny remark foresees the extent to which the Cold War ideology had appropriated poetry. His allusion to the suit to match all the other male Cold Warriors in their civilian "uniforms"—or gray flannel suits—hits right at the center of the Cold War narrative's power to dominate any sphere, including white male dress codes.

The role of the white woman poet in this domesticated, feminized culture was supposed to follow the general female role of the homemaker in her dress, hosiery, high heels, and aprons that the white women's press had been promoting in collaboration with the federal government in the national postwar demobilization of women.[3] Both middle-class women's magazines and the women's staff and sections of newspapers and general magazines supported the new national goals for white women, who were given the task of mothering a new generation and addressing the physical needs of the home and family by procreating and purchasing consumer goods for the "nuclear" family. Given the national context of devaluing women in the workplace in order to promote their return to the home, it is not unexpected that the women's press would also denigrate white women poets in order to promote demobilization.

The Ladies' Home Journal, for example, ran a story entitled "Poet's Kitchen" on Millay in its February 1949 issue that offered its readers the new demobilized patriotic woman-citizen-poet. In fact the message was apparently so successful that Betty Friedan cited it in *The Feminine Mystique* in a long list of examples of the media's transformation of the woman artist into the "happy housewife heroine" (53). Friedan herself had learned to read this stereotype so fully according to cultural norms that she misread this magazine feature as she protested its treatment of Millay. She argued that it showed Millay cooking when Millay was not shown anywhere; moreover, Millay and the magazine staff, with the exception of her friend Alice Blinn, never met (53). Clearly, though, the magazine had achieved its goals of educating women readers, including an ambivalent and resisting reader like Friedan, to domesticate Millay and to flesh out what "Poet's Kitchen" only implied.

The magazine feature article was part of a collaboration by Millay and her husband and manager Eugen Boissevain with their friend Blinn at the magazine, a member of their social circle with their friend Cuthbert, who had handled the World War II propaganda poetry of Millay.[4] Millay received a newly remodeled kitchen in exchange for the magazine article. In a letter dated April 16, 1947, Blinn wrote Boissevain, who handled Millay's business affairs, promising them a new kitchen if they revealed their identities in the feature (Folder 2.10, Millay, VC). As extra enticement, Blinn added that the magazine would likely pay to do more on the kitchen if Millay wrote a domestic poem to accompany the piece (Folder 2.11, Millay, VC).

The magazine's choice of Millay tells us a great deal about her popularity and her political status. She was by this time popularly known as the World War II female patriot poet. This piece places her in a propagandist, patriotic role again as a government-sanctioned role model. Apparently the magazine believed that she could be appropriated successfully to direct and educate its upwardly mobile, educated, middle-class white women readers on how to adapt themselves to their new female roles. In addition to being used to sell demobilization to the women readers of *The Ladies' Home Journal,* Millay is used to promote and to celebrate the American "kitchen" consumerism that Nixon would later use as a war platform in the famous "kitchen debate" against Soviet Premier Nikita S. Khrushchev.

While the magazine article appropriated the public poetic persona of Millay and the public status of her poetry for demobilization and consumerism propaganda, the feature does not show the woman herself. Her physical absence distinguishes her markedly from the national demobilization campaign's employment of photographs of women with public status doing domestic work to encourage women to return to their homes. Photos of well-known actresses like Joan Crawford looking like an average white woman washing her kitchen floor encouraged women to view their household work with pride (May 95). Millay is absent because she refused to be shown, not because the magazine did not want to use a photograph of her.

Letters and negotiations between Boissevain and Blinn indicate Millay's concern not only with having her photograph used in "Poet's Kitchen," but also her words. In a letter dated October 28, 1948, Blinn promised that the piece would not use Millay's photograph or any direct quotes from her. Instead the assigned writer Gladys Taber would work from Blinn's and Boissevain's notes and perhaps a later interview with only Boissevain (Folder 2.11, Millay, VC).

Not only did Millay distance herself physically, but she and her husband controlled the content of the piece as much as possible by insisting that Blinn provide Taber with notes from which to write her feature. A February 2, 1949, letter to Blinn indicates their approval of her notes for Taber as well as the published article (Folder 2.11, Millay, VC). In fact, Millay's uneasiness about the project prompted Blinn to have their mutual friend Cuthbert read every version of the piece at every stage. Blinn added to her description of Cuthbert's role in her letter of January 18, 1949, to Boissevain that she did not see how the feature would harm Millay's reputation as a poet (Folder 2.11, Millay, VC). She concluded by promising nationwide publicity.

Both these negotiations and Millay's refusal to be photographed, interviewed, or quoted, or to write poetry for the piece suggest her ambivalence about the project. One possible political reason for her reluctance was her concern about how her war propaganda poetry had affected her overall poetic reputation. Just one year earlier in 1948 she had told Edmund Wilson that it had been a mistake to write the propaganda poetry (Edel 290). While Millay did not back out of her agreement with the magazine and her friend or refuse the remodeled kitchen, her positioning offers that "yes but no" or "no but yes" that cultural theorists like Gramsci in *Prison Notebooks* and de Certeau in *The Practice of Everyday Life* have suggested constitute an assertion of interwoven contestation and consent. Unlike Blinn, who asserted that she could not see where it would do the poet any harm to be featured in the magazine, Millay appears wary.

Regardless of what occurred in the process of writing the "Poet's Kitchen," it is difficult to avoid reading the published feature piece as part of the larger-scale postwar demobilization "pitch" to women. This "pitch" is used to open the story in the first two paragraphs, giving it the most prominent position in the story's discourse. After placing the reader in a romanticized setting with a Victorian home on a steep hill like the mythic Mount Parnassus, it fetishizes the kitchen in which Millay works and then tells the reader that this is proof that housework is not "beneath" anyone:

> This kitchen is in an old white house at the top of a climbing green hill at the end of a steep and hazardous road. Actually it should be on Mount Parnassus for here at this very sink, in this very kitchen, Edna St. Vincent Millay washes dishes and scours the pots and pans!
>
> Now I expect to hear no more about housework's being "beneath" anyone, for if one of the greatest poets of our day, and any day, can find beauty in simple household tasks, this is the end of the old controversy. (Taber 56)

The magazine piece then proceeds to "sell" the sleek, modern "Cold War" kitchen that allows Millay to do all the housework that servants back in pre–World War II 1923 did, promoting the superiority of postwar domesticity with the woman as the primary domestic. Appropriating

Millay's poetic reputation, the headlines, prominently displayed in boldface in the feature next to the kitchen photo and "before" and "after" architectural drawings, announce:

> Polished as a sonnet . . . Light as a lyric . . .
> Echoing the color of sky and sea she loves . . .
> Must be the kitchen for EDNA ST. VINCENT MILLAY (Taber 56)

As the magazine story continues to invoke the superiority of the new and modern, it becomes clear that anyone with a pre–World War II kitchen was hopelessly outdated. Cold War discourse wished to focus on the new consumerism and growing suburbs and cities. So while Millay might live on a farm, her new consumer goods would reflect her inclusion in this new "containment" world. Nowhere in the article does the "old kitchen" offer anything potentially rewarding or valuable in the new age. In fact it seems ready for the junkyard: "Dark and narrow, the old kitchen was hopelessly inconvenient" (57).

In contrast, the new kitchen "was bright and 'domestic as a plate,'" endorsed and celebrated by the magazine's appropriation of Millay's own published lines of poetry such as "domestic as a plate" in spite of her desire to avoid having her words connected to the feature article (185). By interweaving the new features of the kitchen with references to Millay and her poetry, Taber suggests that Millay's writing and the Cold War culturally correct kitchen legitimize one another.

It appears in the article that poetry's new Muse is the Cold War–era modern kitchen. The feature proclaims, for example, that "poetry is an integral part of living, never an ivory-tower kind of art" (185). We are told that "a wide casement window brought the world outside into the kitchen for a poet who loves the sky" (185). The problem with the "old kitchen" was its impediment to poetry, for "how hard to think of the couplet to close a sonnet when there wasn't a place to put the clean dishes!" (57). The caption praises the breakfast eating nook, citing a Millay poem: "The colorful eating corner makes breakfast a gay affair and provides a place for late supper when there is Conversation at Midnight" (183). The magazine writer then muses further on Millay's poetry and kitchen:

> And I kept thinking how the disciplined
> mind that created sonnets like
>
> Euclid alone has looked on Beauty bare.

or

> Moon, that against the lintel of the west
> Your forehead lean until the gate be swung,

> could attack the details of living as swiftly and
> accurately. (Taber 57)

Moreover, we are told, "Edna had definite ideas about her kitchen. She wanted it streamlined, functional (a sonnet has only fourteen lines, never an extra one) . . ." (Taber 185). After quoting from Millay's lines about herbs, bird calls, and other domestic features, the magazine essay closes with the writer's final employment of Millay and her poetry to sell this domestic scene: "But the poet's kitchen would be a place to work in with contentment, and as I turned to the door I thought of Edna's Winter Night" (185). If readers had any reservations about the importance of a new postwar kitchen in their development as respectable and culturally approved poets like Millay, "Poet's Kitchen" worked diligently to convince them otherwise.

Millay's depiction in "Poet's Kitchen" in the "domesticated" patriotic woman poet's role cast its shadow beyond even her death October 19, 1950. *The Ladies' Home Journal* columnist Dorothy Thompson, for example, described her in the January 1951 issue in the essay "The Woman Poet" as though Millay were the epitome of the U.S. woman poet, against whom all others were to be measured. She told readers: " Miss Millay wrote as a woman. . . . [S]he hardly wrote a lyric which derived its central inspiration from anything but American sights, sounds, smells, tastes, and ideas" (12). This last half of the essay appeared on the same page with a Swift's Premium "tender-grown" chicken ad announcing that "Millions of housewives have acclaimed it THE BIGGEST NEWS IN CHICKENDOM," suggesting that Millay and the new American Cold War domestic world of consumerism with its packaged chicken were solidly intertwined (12).

Thompson encourages this reading of the proper patriotic woman poet loyal to American soil at several other crucial points in the essay as well. Most notably, she separates out Millay for approval from among "the generation of the twenties" who decried "the United States" (12). According to Thompson, Millay traveled extensively but was always homesick: "However tall and wide the tree of her spirit might grow and spread, its roots dug deep in American soil" (12).

This coupling of Millay with U.S. Cold War patriotic domestic culture, however, was not as strong as the journal suggested. Millay did not fully participate in the feature article "Poet's Kitchen." When Millay finally wrote a poem for the magazine, it appeared several issues after the feature, in the November 1949 issue.

Her sonnet "An Ancient Gesture," with its focus on "Penelope" as a contemporary woman wiping her tears on her apron, seems in dialogue with the earlier kitchen feature. It appears to give credibility to this U.S. Cold War domesticated version of Penelope by connecting it to the earlier, classical companion associated with Ulysses and with an ancient Western version of the victory culture. On the other hand, the poem is hardly celebratory with its portrayal of a wife in tears.

Just as instructive as Millay's complex positioning in relation to the magazine project is the magazine's reshaping of her to fit Cold War cultural conventions. Aspects of Millay's biography that would have conflicted with them receded or disappeared. Two important facts did not appear until after her death in the magazine. Her husband did the cooking; and she had no children (Thompson 11-12). While Millay is reported to have been bisexual, no hint of this surfaces anywhere (Walker 177).

Taber's revision of Blinn's notes for the magazine piece about Millay reveal as well that she downplayed Millay's wealth and former household servants in order to indicate that Millay and her husband now did the same kinds of chores as other typical Americans who represented the *Journal* readership. Taber's feature emphasizes that the new Cold War kitchen offers streamlined domestic work that does not require servants any longer (56; 183; 185).

Blinn's "Random Notes on Millay," however, indicates that Millay and her husband may have been ambivalent about the absence of servants. Millay did not take any household responsibility in order to focus completely on her poetry; and the couple ate in the dining room in order to have privacy away from the kitchen. With the loss of servants, Blinn adds, Millay and Boissevain did not eat in the kitchen, but on trays they carried to the living room (Folder 2.10, Millay, VC).

Millay's media refashioning does not represent the experience of all women poets and writers or intellectuals during this time, of course, but her reconstruction did send a cautionary message that women writers were to fold themselves, or allow themselves to be folded, into the mainstream, domestic life of the nation. As Millay's case seems to indicate, the women's press was so determined to construct a woman poet as a cultural role model that the realities of her cultural work and life disappeared in their fictionalizing of an approved domestic pattern.

Bishop faced an equally formidable attempt to insert her into the new Cold War "mold." Yet whereas the magazine feature carved away at Millay until she fit, Bishop's newspaper interviewer both whittled at Bishop and pronounced her unfit. Bishop encountered this journalistic manipulation in her position in Washington, D.C. as the poetry consultant to the Library of Congress in 1949-50. In the feature article "U.S. Poetry Chair Holder Tells How She Courts the Muse," published in the January 8, 1950, issue of *Boston Post Magazine,* reporter Sally Ellis registers ambivalence about Bishop's situation.

The Boston newspaper Sunday magazine was read by an audience of both men and women, so Ellis's goal was to write a woman's piece on Bishop that would be appropriate for her mixed audience. Given the fact that Bishop's public position meant that she was overstepping two gender boundaries simultaneously, her task was formidable. Bishop was not only in a position normally held by white mainstream men, but she had not deferred to the social notion that men should work outside the home, while women return to it. She could have refused the post and allowed for a male consultant.

While no record of this newspaper writing on Bishop exists beyond the printed version in the paper's magazine, Ellis's anxieties about Bishop's gender transgressions are evident in her published writing. Her first strategy is to domesticate and infantilize Bishop and her poetry process, thereby assuring readers that she and the working conditions of poetry are "contained" safely even if what she is doing is also simultaneously "strange." Ellis relies on the literary props of the gothic romance so endemic to New England literature and culture to paint Bishop as another Emily Dickinson or female Brahmin bluestocking out of Henry James's world.

She feminizes poetry and domesticity while pointing to the importance of the strange and secret at the family hearth in language reminiscent of Eve Sedgwick's "language of the closet." She writes:

> Washington, D.C.,—There are strange goings-on up on the attic floor of the Library of Congress!
>
> In a 24-foot office that looks so much like a Beacon Hill drawing-room that you expect tea and bread-and-butter sandwiches to be served any minute, an attractive young woman sits at her desk piecing scraps of paper together.
>
> . . . Sometimes it will be a week or again six months before she assembles all her scraps on her desktop and puts them together like a jigsaw puzzle.
>
> Then Elizabeth Bishop has a poem!

"There's nothing at all complicated about it," she explained; "it's like making a map." (Monteiro 3)

Even though Bishop is working in a publicly visible professional space inside the nation's Library of Congress across from the Capitol, Ellis describes her as a writer in a private, domestic space, tucked away in the attic and isolated from the rest of the library. One can not help but think in the post–Cold War 2000s of Victorian images of the "madwoman in the attic" that scholars Gilbert and Gubar have popularized.

Ellis's domestication of Bishop also follows social class norms in Cold War "containment" culture, which encouraged the nation's citizens to aspire to middle- and upper-class, white Anglo-Saxon Protestant values. So the feature places Bishop within an emblematical setting of this world: a tea scene in a Beacon Hill drawing room of the Boston Brahmins that could have appeared in a James novel. Ellis's reference to being served tea indicates that Bishop would preside over tea, but that someone else would do the actual domestic preparation and serving work.

When the magazine story refers to Bishop piecing together poetry, it sounds like a parlor pastime to be put away for tea guests in the afternoon when her nurturing feminine role is brought out for the publicly sanctioned role of socializing. The feature promotes cultural norms for women further in its ambivalent description of Bishop as a "quiet" and "self-effacing" woman from Worcester, Massachusetts, who is "a poet and not an ordinary one either" (3).

Of even greater importance to readers in McCarthy-dominated 1950 was the issue of Bishop's patriotism. As a government employee, the national poetry consultant was expected to be intensely patriotic—or at least an anti-Communist liberal who could pass security clearance. So the story focuses on Bishop's interest in mapmaking and her equation of poetry-writing with mapping. In a Cold War political discourse that saw its mission as the remapping of the globe in the image of the United States, such an avocation would seem to place her writing directly in synchronization with the nation's. Later, the feature indicates that Bishop owes her poetic success largely to her World War II poetry: "Her work received wide recognition after the publication of a poem 'Roosters' in a special poetry number of *The New Republic*" (4).

The feature did not pursue Bishop's politics much further, however. Such an oversight would seem to conform to the notion that U.S. women, even the occasional woman in the public eye, were expected to be apolitical. In Bishop's case this worked to her advantage. Either Ellis did not research Bishop's background or chose to omit, for example, that some of Bishop's publishers had been liberal to leftist. In fact some of her allies faced questioning for their earlier leftist thinking. Jarrell, for example, found that his publication in such journals created problems when he was nominated later for the post. While Ellis listed *Partisan Review* among Bishop's credentials, she did not pursue her substantial relationship with it. Between 1935 and 1952, Bishop published 19 pieces of identified poetry and prose in *Partisan Review,* although by the early 1950s she had begun to publish in *The New Yorker* (Harrison 222).

Ellis did not know, of course, that her story actually was about a woman who would have been considered a poor security risk and likely dismissed from her job. Bishop actually did not conform to what Maxine Kumin said was expected from a woman poet in the job when she took it many years later, long after Cold War roles for women had begun to unravel. Her remarks are a barometer of how confining the Library of Congress job must have been for Bishop. Kumin said she was expected to be a very safe, heterosexual, middle-class, middle-aged woman poet, "the kind who wasn't going to disgrace anybody" (McGuire 389).

As is well known now but not discussed then, Bishop was an antimilitarist, an orphan, a U.S. citizen still deeply attached to her childhood home in Canada, a lesbian, an alcoholic, a sufferer of autoimmune and mental health disorders with a family history of mental illness, including a mother who suffered a nervous breakdown and was hospitalized for most of her adult life. Nor did Ellis know that in 1951 Bishop would travel to Brazil and not return to the United States until the mid–1960s, when the United States began to open up culturally and socially and to manifest its political divisiveness on the Cold War policy of "containment."

While Bishop escaped derision in the Ellis feature story for many aspects of her subject positioning, her status as a single working woman was treated ambivalently. Ellis portrays Bishop as an unattractive worker, conforming directly to the views of the national demobilization project. Ellis states that Bishop is a "38–year-old" consultant in poetry at a time when it was considered important to provide a woman's age in news stories (3). Yet there is no mention of husband or family. In fact, by this point in the story the "attractive young woman" in paragraph two has been called a "quiet," "self-effacing," "not ordinary" woman who "sweats out" her struggle with the Muse, hardly an attractive but perhaps acceptable woman figure for official Cold War culture.

In addition, Ellis's descriptions seem to conform to the culture's treatment of the unmarried woman as undesirable. The influential psychological team of Marynia Farnham and Ferdinand Lundberg, for example, declared that "all unmarried women should be barred by law from having anything to do with the teaching of children on the grounds of theoretical (usually real) emotional incompetence. . . . Such women are by nature unhappy and destructive" (370–71).

Although no direct response by Bishop to this feature has been found, the experience with Ellis undoubtedly contributed significantly to her protestation of *Vogue's* depiction of her with Jarrell and Peter Viereck in 1953. She complained about the use of the words "coldness and precision" and condemned the description as a cliché for women poets in her April 25, 1953, letter to her friend Pearl Kazin Bell (*OA* 262). As Bishop's complaint testifies, the women's press succeeded in devaluing and defacing women poets and women's poetry.

Both magazine features on Millay and Bishop contributed as well to a climate of anxiety about women's gender and sexual behavior in early Cold War culture. Widespread public debate over female heterosexual behavior and contraception ensued throughout the 1950s with the Kinsey Report, Planned Parenthood, Margaret Sanger's pioneering birth control work, and testing for an oral contraceptive.

In addition, female homosexual behavior was criminalized. In February 1950, shortly after the feature on Bishop was published, McCarthy launched his major anti-Communist offensive. Alan Bérubé has called it "the most aggressive attack on homosexual employees that had ever taken place in the federal government" (265). He reports that after Under Secretary of State John Peurifoy testified on February 28, 1950, before a Senate Committee investigating the loyalty of government employees that most of the 91 State Department employees dismissed as security risks were homosexuals, new antihomosexual activity took place in Washington almost weekly. The impact was severe. From a dismissal of an average of five homosexuals each month, the rate grew to more than sixty per month (266, 269). Not only was the committee seeking the dismissal of homosexuals, but it wanted them to be seen as potential Communists so that the public would begin to see the term "homosexual" and "Communist" as interchangeable (Edelman, "Tearooms and Sympathy" 263–84).

Bérubé states that "by the late 1940s . . . the ability of gay men and lesbians to blend into normal life became increasingly difficult as the attention of the nation's media, government officials, and church leaders turned toward issues of conformity and deviance." He adds that "as families were reunited and struggled to put their lives back together after the war, articles, books, advertisements, and the media promoted idealized versions of the nuclear family, heterosexuality, and traditional gender roles in the home and in the workplace" (257-58). Thus heterosexuality and the nuclear family came to represent the new Cold War national narrative.

Bishop's friend Mary Meigs offers insight into what it meant for her generation of lesbians:

> Elizabeth and I belonged to a generation of women who were terrified by the idea of being known as lesbians, and for Elizabeth as poet, the lesbian label would have been particularly dangerous. One of the side effects of lesbians' fear of being known to the world was our fear of being known to each other, so that kind of caution was exercised (certainly it was by Elizabeth) that no longer seems necessary today. (Fountain 86)

Negative cultural pressures for women writers were strong enough that Diana Trilling later decried women's anxieties about speaking out in fiction in a statement that seems relevant to women poets, and especially Bishop herself:

> If we look at the work of our most talented women writers of fiction, we see how commonly it is obscured by private reference, hidden patterns of reasoning, excessive discursion, over-modification of ideas, and other forms of non-declarativeness. Individual temperaments cannot account for something this endemic in culture. We must conclude that the American woman has reason to fear speaking. (53)

One of the reasons that women like Bishop faced formidable social problems is that the Cold war national narrative had only one definition of American women after 1949: the housewife-mother. As Friedan argued in her study of women in this period, *The Feminine Mystique:*

> In an earlier time, the image of woman was also split in two—the good, pure woman on the pedestal, and the whore of the desires of the flesh. The split in the new image opens a different fissure—the feminine woman, whose goodness includes the desires of the flesh, and the career woman, whose evil includes every desire of the separate self. The new feminine morality story is the exorcising of the forbidden career dream . . . the dream of independence, the discontent of spirit, and even the feeling of a separate identity. . . . With the career woman out of the way, the housewife with interests in the community becomes the devil to be exorcised. Even PTA takes on a suspect connotation. (46-47)

As the 1950s unfolded, women of letters, as Eugenia Kaledin has pointed out in her study of women in this decade, tried to keep options open for women: to help their women readers envision being women with their own dreams (122). The roster of literary women includes but is not limited to Flannery O'Connor, Eudora Welty, Caroline Gordon, Carson McCullers, Ellen Glasgow, Hortense Callisher, Grace Paley, Tillie Olsen, Kay Boyle, Shirley Jackson, Jean Kerr, Phyllis McGinley, Mary McCarthy, Edna Ferber, Fannie Hurst, Pearl Buck, Ann Petry, Marianne Moore, Louise Bogan, Josephine Miles, May Swenson, May Sarton, Gwendolyn Brooks, Muriel Rukeyser, Audre Lorde, Adrienne Rich, Denise Levertov, Anne Sexton, Sylvia Plath, Diane DiPrima, Lillian Hellman, Lorraine Hansberry, and Dorothy Parker.

But such a flowering also was kept pruned. The problem of justifying women with careers as writers continued through the 1950s. Writing women often found themselves depicted as "just housewives" or otherwise domestically "contained." The *McCall's* April 1956 issue, for instance, features Shirley Jackson, Jean Kerr, and Phyllis McGinley commemorating domesticity. *The Ladies' Home Journal* negotiated the issue of how to handle women writers by publishing sentimental fiction that followed the Cold War script for women but also poetry by such poets as Moore, Sarton, Plath, and Rich.

Given a right-leaning Cold War national narrative proscribing and monitoring strict adherence to guidelines on gender and sexuality and cultural production in the struggle against Communism, it is not surprising that anxiety and self-doubt overwhelmed Bishop as soon as she considered the poetry consultancy and her own personal Cold War narrative. She faced, for example, the thorny problem of how to manage the amorous advances of Lowell, who mentored—or maneuvered—her into the center of cultural power by sponsoring her for the Washington poetry position as well as a residency at the prestigious art colony Yaddo in Saratoga Springs, New York. Then she was compelled to negotiate the political turmoil in the wake of his accusation in early 1949 that Elizabeth Ames, the executive director of Yaddo, was a Communist as well the controversial awarding of the Bollingen Prize to Pound while he was under house arrest in St. Elizabeth's Hospital in Washington. While she was coping with Lowell's actions and cultural politics on one hand, Bishop also was attempting to manage her declining health and a volatile personal life.

Bishop's lifelong friendship with Lowell began in January 1947 when Jarrell introduced them at his apartment in New York City while he was serving as literary editor of *The Nation* in Margaret Marshall's absence

(Travisano, *Midcentury Quartet* 163).[5] Lowell responded enthusiastically to Bishop; and in a letter of February 20, he recommended her poetry to Louis Untermeyer for the next anthology of American poets that he was compiling (Mariani 149, 477). In mid-October she stopped in Washington, D.C. on her way to visit Key West and recorded for Lowell in his position as poetry consultant, a post he had begun just that fall (Fountain 101).

In May 1948 Lowell began pursuing Bishop more avidly. She returned to Washington to record again for Lowell at his invitation; and he arranged for her and her pet canary to stay with his fiancée at the time, Carley Dawson (Fountain 101; Mariani 164). On this visit he took her to visit Pound, about whom he was very enthusiastic. Bishop was mystified by Pound's writing, but she told Lowell that she was "really endlessly grateful" that he had taken her with him (Millier 199).

He also saw her shortly afterwards in New York even though he had promised Dawson that he would not see another girlfriend named Gertrude because of their engagement (Mariani 164). On June 9 Lowell wrote to Bishop to tell her how much he enjoyed her company (Folder 7.2, VC). Then on July 2, he offered to write Bishop a letter to recommend her for residency at Yaddo, where he was planning to stay after he finished his tenure as poetry consultant, and wanted Moore to write on her behalf as well (Folder 7.2, VC). By early August, Lowell's divorce from Jean Stafford had been finalized, and he went to see Bishop in Wiscasset, Maine, where she was staying with her friend (and possible lover) Tom Wanning (Mariani 165–67). Lowell had just broken his engagement to Dawson, but she decided to visit Bishop as well at the same time. The visit ended in a fiasco, with Dawson and Wanning leaving Bishop to manage Lowell on her own.

The next time that Bishop seems to have seen Lowell was November at the elite Bard Conference, where they were among the nation's major and upcoming poets and writers, including Lowell's next wife Hardwick (Fountain 101; Mariani 171). Shortly afterward both attended Eliot's lecture on Poe at the Library of Congress, Bishop with Pauline Hemingway and Jane Dewey. Bishop and Hemingway spent the night at Dawson's apartment so that Bishop could lunch the next day with Lowell and Auden. She missed the lunch because she became intoxicated and spent five days in a detoxification center (Mariani 173). Lowell invited her to visit him during his second residency at Yaddo in December, but she refused, heading for Key West instead (Fountain 109). This rejection seemed to defuse the relationship sufficiently; and Lowell turned his attentions to Hardwick. Years later, Lowell said he had wanted to propose to her that summer.

Bishop felt that her anxiety attacks over the Library of Congress position were formidable in January 1949 when she shared them by letter with Lowell after learning in Key West about the post and its salary of $5,700. She was especially worried about giving public readings (*OA* 180-181). Lowell tried to soothe her concerns and said that the workload amounted to only about two days a week (Fountain 110). There were few duties. The consultant advised the Library of Congress on holdings in poetry, organized meetings of the Society of Fellows, acted as a clearinghouse of information about poetry in the government, and visited Pound regularly at St. Elizabeth's Hospital (a written duty at the time) (Millier 210, 220).

If she found it difficult to prepare herself to manage a job for the first time, the year's Yaddo uproar and the Bollingen Award to Pound leading up to her assumption of her duties in the fall could only have exacerbated her concerns. Lowell's charges at Yaddo were so painful for the artists' colony that the "moment" continues to be described as "wrenching" by as recent an article as "A Peek at Life in an Artists' Retreat" published in *The New York Times* on July 19, 1999, which states that "the poet Robert Lowell plunged Yaddo into the hysteria of the Communist witch hunts" with his accusations against Ames, who was cleared and remained in her post until 1969 (Dobrzynski B1, B4). In addition, Pound's anti-Semitic writings and broadcasts from Fascist Italy during World War II, which led to his arrest, indictment for treason, and confinement at St. Elizabeth's Hospital, continue to incite as much furor today when he is nominated for an honor as it did when he was awarded the Bollingen. In October 1999 the dean of the Cathedral of St. John the Divine in New York City overruled the Poets' Corners electors' decision to honor Pound with a place in the Poets' Corner of the cathedral because of his anti-Semitism and pro-Fascism as well as "the lingering pain they have caused members of the cathedral's congregation" (Dinitia Smith A17, A20).

For Bishop who already abhorred militarism, the story at Yaddo must have been a lesson in how military politics can intervene in the arts as citizen-artists capitulate to its authority. It began on February 11, while Bishop was traveling with her friend, Pauline Hemingway's sister Virginia Pfeiffer, in Haiti. The former Yaddo resident Agnes Smedley, a journalist and novelist who supported the Chinese Communists, was accused on the front page of *The New York Times* by General Douglas MacArthur of being a contact for a Soviet spy ring (Hamilton 143). The army admitted in *The Times* on February 19 that it had no evidence against Smedley so the paper retracted its earlier story and Smedley thanked the army for clearing her name the next day. Lowell—along with Hardwick, Flannery O'Connor, and Edward

Maisel—nevertheless asked for Ames's dismissal as executive director of Yaddo (MacKinnon 330, 335).

They believed Ames was implicated with Smedley because she had allowed Smedley to extend her stay at Yaddo beyond the awarded time (MacKinnon 330). Smedley had lived at Yaddo from 1943 until March 1948. Yaddo had taken pride in its anti-Fascist hospitality so Smedley, whom Ames assumed to be a Marxist, was offered a residency (Hamilton 143). Ames had disagreed with Smedley about politics and had asked her to leave, but Lowell ignored this information (MacKinnon 320). When the FBI interviewed Hardwick, Lowell, Maisel, and O'Connor, the only guests in residence, they said that they felt uneasy at Yaddo (Hamilton 144).

On February 26, Lowell, representing all four guests, demanded that the board of directors of Yaddo dismiss Ames immediately, using the Cold War rhetoric of disease in comparing Yaddo to a body and calling Ames "a diseased organ, chronically poisoning the whole system" (Hamilton 143-45, 148, 151-52; Mariani 178). In addition, Lowell threatened to go public with his demand.

To support his call for Ames's dismissal, he named other writers whom he said supported his views, but without having spoken with them. Bishop appeared on the list with Leonie Adams, Auden, Berryman, Blackmur, Bogan, Eliot, William Empson, James Farrell, Robert Fitzgerald, Frost, Jarrell, Moore, Katherine Anne Porter, J. F. Powers, John Crowe Ransom, Santayana, Schwartz, Karl Shapiro, Stafford, Tate, Peter Taylor, Robert Penn Warren, and William Carlos Williams (Hamilton 145; Meeting transcript, February 26, 1949, Malcolm Cowley Papers, Newberry Library). Hardwick wrote Bishop three letters telling her about Lowell's claims (Millier 212-13). Lowell's actions inflamed the cultural community, particularly those members associated with Yaddo who feared that its reputation would be damaged by the Communist accusations. A master politician throughout his career who knew how to manage politics to his advantage, Lowell offered a considerable challenge (Axelrod, "Robert Lowell and the Cold War" 339-61; Flanzbaum, 49-57).

The board did not fire Ames. She resigned and entered a nursing home immediately. Her secretary, who had been an FBI informant for five years listening to conversations at Yaddo and mailing names and addresses for investigation, also resigned (Hamilton 146; 148).

On March 21, a group of former Yaddo guests and Ames supporters, including Harvey Breit, John Cheever, Eleanor Clark, Malcolm Cowley, Alfred Kazin, Carson McCullers, Kappo Phelan, Porter, and Schwartz, circulated a petition on her behalf (Hamilton 484; March 21, 1949 Petition,

Malcolm Cowley Papers, Newberry Library). In the letter they repudiated Lowell's charges. They sent 75 copies of the petition. By March 26, they had 51 endorsements, and Ames was exonerated at the meeting of the board of directors at Yaddo. While they confirmed Ames, they were critical about the length of guest stays. Lowell was shocked by all of this, especially by the fact that some of his friends supported Ames (Hamilton 151-52).

Also on March 26 as Ames was being exonerated, Lowell seemed to be accelerating in his liberal anti-Stalinism. He heckled such Soviet participants as composer Dmitri Shostakovich at the Cultural & Scientific Conference for World Peace at the Waldorf-Astoria Hotel in New York along with McCarthy, Macdonald, and Hook. Many U.S. speakers at the conference blamed the United States and the Soviet Union equally for escalating Cold War tensions, including Leonard Bernstein, Aaron Copland, DuBois, Mailer, and Smedley (Axelrod, "Robert Lowell and the Cold War," 344-45).

In March, while the Yaddo scene was heating up, Bishop went into a hospital in Miami for problems with alcoholism from Key West (Fountain 112). On March 22 she wrote Dr. Anny Baumann, who had begun treating her, worried about the upcoming Washington job and other problems (Folder 4.2, VC).

The next month the aftermath at Yaddo began to take an unusual turn as Tate and Robert Fitzgerald stepped forward to try to help Lowell. Tate reprimanded Hardwick and O'Connor in a letter dated April 4, 1949, criticizing them for having abetted Lowell at Yaddo. He was especially emphatic about the fact that as women they did not know how to evaluate the situation in public terms (Hamilton 156). Apparently he felt that others would have stopped Lowell from proceeding as he had. Then Fitzgerald tried to explain Lowell in an open letter dated May 26, 1949, emphasizing the fact that all four accusers had felt uneasy at Yaddo (Hamilton 484).

Lowell's mental health had begun to unravel, and he was hospitalized during that spring and summer. He was not able to function fully again until Christmas, although he married Hardwick during this time and accepted a teaching position at the University of Iowa. Then after Iowa he prepared for a trip to Europe while the Korean War began and stayed almost two years there (Hamilton 162-88).

This period was also very difficult for Bishop. In May and June she was in the hospital, "isolated" at Blythedale in Greenwich, Connecticut, for alcoholism treatment and apparently mumps (Fountain 112; *OA* 185). She recovered in time to stay at Yaddo, which was still in turmoil over the Lowell charges. She reported that she found the experience too intense (*OA*

186). Her alcoholism continued to be a problem for her, and she feared that she was disintegrating like Hart Crane and that everyone would give up on her (*OA* 188). She told MacIver that she was trying to stay sober in a letter of July 3, 1949. Ames had helped her, and Bishop planned to see a physician friend of Ames's, but indicated that she would be very careful about what she said (*OA* 186).

Bishop was extremely anxious about how Lowell would view her stay at Yaddo. On July 31, 1949, she wrote MacIver that she did not know if she was among Communists or not and that she was scared to write Lowell about where she was (*OA* 248). On August 12, 1949, she seemed relieved that she had received his approval for her stay at Yaddo; but by this time she also had decided that Ames would never get over his attack, and she was troubled by his lack of remorse about that (*OA* 260). Bishop's evaluation of Ames's troubled situation is accurate, for Ames had gone into the nursing home in distress (Hamilton 151-52). Her concern about Lowell's lack of remorse is also remarkably prescient about his selective amnesia, or loss of memory due to medical treatments for his manic depression. Years later he told Alfred Kazin, who had supported Ames against Lowell, that he "had forgotten the Yaddo episode" (Kazin 205).

While negotiating the anguish that followed the Yaddo "moment," Bishop also needed to manage the divisive politics over the Library of Congress Bollingen Prize to Pound that was announced February 20, the same day that Smedley was cleared of charges, by *The New York Times* with the headline "Pound, In Mental Clinic, Wins Prize for Poetry, Penned in Treason Cell" (Hamilton 143). The committee of judges included Conrad Aiken, Bogan, Auden, Eliot, Warren, Shapiro, Leonie Adams, Katherine Chapin, Katherine Anne Porter, Willard Thorp, Tate, and Lowell, who said that the prize was based on poetic achievement only (Hamilton 142). But the prize was viewed as controversial immediately.

The job in Washington was very much on her mind, for she wrote from the hospital that she had read about the library in a recent *New Yorker*. She also said that she was worried about all the typing at the library and wished to avoid writing the 5,000–word essay on her innermost thoughts that John Ciardi wanted (*OA* 186).

Anxieties about beginning her post in Washington continued to grow while Bishop was at Yaddo. She reported that everyone had told her so much about how well Adams had handled everything that she was certain that she would fail and would rather not do the work (*OA* 188). Indeed in another letter she said that intended to never do another review, recording, or reading. Above all, she wanted to resign from the job in Washington

(*OA* 190). In addition, she admitted to having difficulty in adjusting to the fact that she would be living in a boardinghouse in Washington (*OA* 190).

Bishop's growing unhappiness with her poetry consultancy parallels the fiery debate over the awarding of the Bollingen to Pound, initiated by *The Saturday Review of Literature.* Yet she failed to mention the growing heat generated by it. Her name appeared nowhere in the furor that lasted through 1949, but her job positioned her right in the middle of it. On June 11, Robert Hillyer protested the selection of Pound in an essay entitled "Treason's Strange Fruit: The Case of Ezra Pound and the Bollingen Award," castigating the decision because of Pound's pro-Fascist activities that led to his federal indictment for treason (9-11; 28). The appropriation of Holiday's song "Strange Fruit" for the title links Pound's politics firmly to racial violence both abroad and on the home front and prepares the way for the essay's inquiries into the Fascism and racism of "The Pisan Cantos," for which he had received the award, and the use of the prize to counter-balance the charges of treason. Accompanying the essay was the editorial "Ezra Pound and the Bollingen Award" denouncing the award to Pound. In the follow-up essay on June 18, 1949, Hillyer's "New Priesthood" casti-gates the argument of "art for art's sake" used on behalf of Pound and crit-icizes his poetry for its "meretricious verbiage" (7).

The July 2 issue printed the full letter of Luther H. Evans, Librarian of Congress, responding to the two Hillyer pieces and the magazine's editor-ial, in its editorial pages. Evans defended the prize jury's character and their decision in the interest of scholarly freedom, while personally regarding the choice of the cantos as "unfortunate" (21). The magazine's editors responded by bolstering their views on Pound's politics again (22-23). On July 30, the magazine printed the official letter of the prize jury protesting the magazine's charges against them and replied by asking for a defense of the cantos as poetry (22).

During the fall of 1949, the uproar continued. Debate reached a climax with the December 17 publication in *The Nation* of a letter (with the cap-tion "A Prepared Attack") circulated by Berryman in defense of the prize jury and signed by 84 people that *The Saturday Review of Literature* had declined to print.(598-99). Margaret Marshall wrote an editorial against the magazine's decision under the caption "'The Saturday Review' Unfair to Literature." *The Saturday Review of Literature* defended its decision in its December 31 issue, stating that the letter (which it said had 72 signatures) had been sent after it had closed the letters section of the discussion and the letter had been published by *Poetry Magazine* in a pamphlet condemning the magazine's views, and outlined the demand that Berryman include the names of persons who had refused to sign the letter, which he had declined to do (22).

Meanwhile, a joint congressional committee abolished all further Library of Congress awards and moved the Bollingen Prize to Yale University. When the next winner, Wallace Stevens, was announced, *Time* contrasted him sharply with Pound, "longtime tubthumper for Mussolini and fascism," by depicting Stevens as a poets' poet who quietly built up his reputation while working every day beginning promptly at 8:15 as vice president of the Hartford Accident & Indemnity Company ("The Laurels" 36).

Although Bishop likely thought that her difficulties with the Pound award were over during her tenure at the library, the furor over Pound reemerged when Lowell accepted the National Book Award on her behalf in 1969 while she was in Brazil. In a March 11, 1970, letter he told her that he had stated at the dinner that the nominations list had omitted Pound, who had just published a book, and then read her poem about Pound, "Visits to St. Elizabeths." After he had finished speaking, Kenneth Rexroth had announced that he wanted to sever himself from Lowell's anti-Semitic Fascist performance (Folder 9.4, VC).

While her experiences with Yaddo and the Bollingen uproar as well as with Lowell aggravated her anxiety and her illnesses, Bishop also was trying to move ahead in her shattered personal life. She had decided to leave Stevens and Key West and temporarily lived in New York. But she was rootless, visiting or traveling with friends when she was not in a hospital until the Yaddo colony and then a boardinghouse in Washington, D.C. During this time she also decided to distance herself from Wanning, who remained a lifelong friend. A letter from Pauline Hemingway of June 4, 1948, asks Bishop if she is engaged yet, as though some kind of engagement to Wanning, or even perhaps to Lowell, might be expected (17.9, VC). While it is not clear exactly what kind of relationship she had with Wanning or Lowell, no more men seem prominent in her life after this, suggesting that she had come to understand that she needed to live her life as a lesbian. She continued her close relationships with Pauline Hemingway and especially her sister Virginia Pfeiffer, who traveled with her to Haiti in early 1949. She began to see more of Jane Dewey, whom she had known since early Key West, and stayed in touch with Margaret Miller and Louise Crane.

Her relationship with Dewey became intense during this time. She stayed with Dewey in Maryland on her way to Key West in November 1948, visiting Edgar Allan Poe's grave in Baltimore in the rain and attending Eliot's lecture at the Library of Congress with both Dewey and Hemingway (Fountain 110; Mariani 172-73). She also visited Dewey in December 1948 (*OA* 179). While she was at Yaddo, she wrote MacIver on July 19, 1949, that a recent phone call from Dewey had helped her to feel better (*OA* 190). And while she was drinking again by July 31, a letter from Dewey boosted her spirits (*OA* 190).

Only several weeks later in September, Bishop emerged from Yaddo to embark upon her first job, a highly visible government post in a field of cultural production that was fractured violently by Lowell's attack on Ames and the Bollingen Prize award to Pound. A deeply private woman, Bishop must have recoiled at the thought of finding herself in any kind of limelight, much less as a major actor in a highly fraught cultural controversy. For if she was at the center, she must have feared that surely investigators would uncover her lesbian life, her alcoholism, her politics; and then she, too, would find herself charged in the newspapers and facing public dissection.

Bishop did not suffer this fate. She was a public model of propriety and rectitude. These traits, interestingly, were attributed to her "Canadian" identity. "I didn't know if Elizabeth was American or not," recalls Joseph Frank, who became acquainted with her during her year as poetry consultant in Washington, D.C.:

> It wasn't clear because she spoke so much about Nova Scotia. I had the feeling that she didn't feel at home in this country somehow, that she was rather alien from that point of view [because] these early years had shaped her sensibility in such a way. She wasn't a regular fellow—she was more Canadian and more English than she was American. There was not this kind of American casualness about her as a person. She was aware of that. She traced it to the different kind of bringing up she had had. She was much more rigorous in some deep moral and social sense than the ordinary American. (Barry, *Elizabeth Bishop* 10)

Even more important, however, Bishop's behavior as described by Frank suggests that she was continuing to distance herself from mainstream national American culture. Indeed, Bishop wrote in her 1950 diary that this was her worst year so far. Much later, in a letter of February 25, 1965, to Jarrell, when the nation was challenging the Vietnam conflict and the culture of "containment," she brought up her expatriatism. She told him that he was a real American and that the nation in his poetry was much more real than anything that she had encountered in the country. While she found the term "American" loaded with many undesirable meanings, he made her feel almost nostalgic and disloyal. But then she added that she had always been an expatriate (*OA* 433).

Although she had been brought to the United States from Canada during the Great War, she had retained her love and loyalty for the nation of Canada. During World War II, she watched her beloved Key West disappear with the installation of a U.S. naval base. Now in her new job in Washington in 1949–50, she faced the prospect of further losses to yet another war—the Cold War and, soon, the Korean War. Even though she held onto her U.S. citizenship and was never overtly threatened with its loss, the events of her year in Washington undoubtedly made her realize that she was "outside" American culture. She was an "international," a displaced person with a diasporic, hybrid identity that complicated even the usual terms of "mother country" and "country of settlement." She had been taken to her legal U.S. "mother country" from her Canadian "country of settlement." She had reached the national cultural center of power in Washington, D.C., in the early Cold War "containment" victory narrative during 1949 and 1950, only to find that it could offer no real home or "mother country" to her.

For her, the year was nearly disabling—but not quite.[6] In addition to the ongoing uproar over the Pound poetry award, she missed work frequently due to asthma attacks and alcoholic illness and underwent treatment during Christmas week in a Saratoga, New York, hospital (Millier, "The Prodigal," 59–61). She also was preoccupied with the need to find better living arrangements. She decided that living at a boardinghouse would not work in September and began looking for an apartment or another living situation; but she did not move until April (*OA* 194).

But with the orientation of Adams and the guidance of the office secretary Phyllis Armstrong, who knew when chores needed to be done and nudged her to do them and served sherry to callers, Bishop was able to manage some of the workload. She hosted a tea party in December for Frost, about the time that *The Nation* published the list of writers supporting the Pound prize jury. Sandburg surprised everyone by showing up, but they acted very awkwardly and did not speak to one another (*OA* 197).

Although she focused on their behavior, she did not mention that the letter of support for the Pound prize also might have cast a pall over her social plans. Her name is conspicuously absent from the list. Was she recovering from her illnesses while the signatures were gathered and then submitted for publication and therefore not approached? Did Bishop feel that her government employee status meant that she could not sign the letter? Was she fearful of appearing on any list that might be targeted easily for investigation? Did she want to stay out of controversy? Did she disagree with the choice of Pound? Was she deferring to her boss at the Library of Congress, Luther Evans, who had responded to the debate?

No evidence of her thoughts about this letter of support has been found. But, given her thoughts about Pound, which we will consider in the next chapter, before she assumed her position and while she was required to visit him, she was very uncomfortable with his selection. She probably found the publication of the letter to be very stressful since it put her position in the limelight, exactly what she wished to avoid, where the question of her own civil liberties was at stake.

Her year was very quiet on the whole. She also held a business meeting of the Library of Congress fellows and a Rudolf Serkin concert (*OA* 197). She avoided public appearances as much as possible and declined an invitation from John Malcolm Brinnin to read at the YMHA Poetry Center in New York in February (*OA* 198). The highlight of her year was Dylan Thomas's reading on May 8, which she had begun arranging in October (*OA* 195).

One of her other most difficult moments was Jarrell's failure to win the job after her. He had nurtured high hopes of succeeding her when Aiken did. She tried to console him and said she was sick of poetry as big business, just as he was by this time (*OA* 201-2).

Wilbur observed during this era that the U. S. poet "showed less of the conventional romantic defiance, somewhat less of the bitterness of the wallflower; he is increasingly disposed to think of himself as a citizen" (115-16). But this was obviously not an easy task for Bishop, who watched the nation's growing military-industrial culture under construction through the window of her poetry consultancy office at the Library of Congress, where she looked directly at the Capitol dome as the Cold War national narrative constricted her poetic and private life. Succeeding Tate, Warren, Bogan, Shapiro, Lowell, and Adams in the position established by MacLeish during the WPA days under Roosevelt, she did not find the view as pleasing as had Shapiro, who wrote Lowell that it was one of the most beautiful in Washington (Hamilton 154). She found her year to be more like Lowell's year, which he had compared to his imprisonment as a conscientious objector during World War II (Hamilton 169).

Courtesy of the Library of Congress.

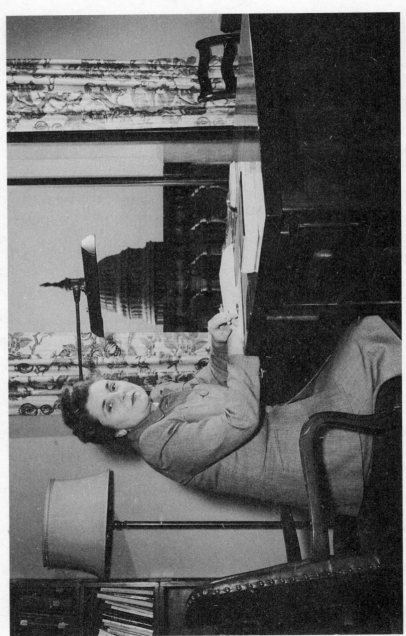

Courtesy of the Library of Congress.

Courtesy of the Library of Congress.

Chapter 6 ⌒

FROM A POET'S WINDOW: WASHINGTON, 1949-1950

With her poetry consultancy office window overlooking Congress, Bishop enjoyed a highly privileged insider's view of emerging Cold War culture in spite of her secret outsider status. She literally could see the Capitol every work day as the national government began to formulate the Cold War and to commit the nation to the Korean War in 1950. She thus had a "forced" eyewitness view of the Cold War's "arrival" in, or invasion of, daily U.S. life. Official Washington rhetoric overflowed with visions of its postwar national power to vanquish Communism and to save the world. The U.S. international news magazine *Time* reported an example of this emerging dominant national discourse in its May 29, 1950, issue as it quoted a government spokesman on Cold War "containment" policy in its news report, "The Nation: The Good War":

It is the only war in history where the question of destruction doesn't enter into it at all. Everything we are doing is building up. We have rebuilt Europe, not destroyed it. . . . Now, if we carry on a smart, resourceful, cold war, the kind of war free people can carry on, Russia will be contained. . . . All we have to do is carry on intelligently, and at extremely low cost, the political, economic, military and informational measures already under way. ("The Nation" 1)

Official Washington saw itself in mythical proportions and persuaded most of its citizens, as well as much of the world, to view it this way because of its cultural hegemonic dominance—its ability to saturate the global culture with the same message reiterated by cultural producers across both "high" and "popular" cultural forms of production ranging from poetry to comic books. Bishop, however, was skeptical about this Cold War idea of "building . . . intelligently."

Bishop was visibly and officially silent about this victory culture and narrative while in office. Yet her silence at a time when the nation was not only returning to "hot" war through the Korean War but laying the foundation of a nuclear-dominated militarized domestic and foreign policy seems too deafening to overlook. Her very absence from the public site/sight of "speech" when she was at the center of cultural power in Washington asks us to ponder and probe what might be behind it, to consider more closely what might be omitted from the "received" mainstream history and national memory of this period, and to search out what has been submerged. What did she need to negotiate as a poet? What were her views? How did Bishop negotiate her uneasy positioning within this victory narrative that also was quickly categorizing her lesbianism under the category of treasonous, Communist enemy? How could the poet who had written the "V-Day August 14th, 1945" fragment speak in a public arena?

Given MacLeish's World War II propaganda efforts, Millay's reappearance in the public eye as the ideal patriotic woman poet in demobilization, Pound's hospital imprisonment on charges of national treason as well as his recent prize from the Library of Congress, and Yaddo's disarray after the charges against its director Elizabeth Ames, one would have expected the holder of Bishop's office to feel more than the usual pressure to produce public patriotic poetry in order to maintain government support for the office of poetry consultant. Negotiating the expectations that a woman poet, especially a woman poet in the nation's office of poetry, should function as a Penelope figure required extraordinary rhetorical manipulation.

In many respects, Bishop was alone and isolated in her poetry post. In addition, she was one of the few who were taking the Korean War seriously while it would seem that Americans were encouraged to "forget" the war and did. Another notable exception was the poet Sylvia Plath, who published her anti-Korean War poem "Bitter Strawberries" in *The Christian Science Monitor* shortly after the war began and used three female voices to represent varying war positions. A female boss advocates war; a woman who may be a mother, girlfriend, or wife of a man of draft age offers conflicted assent to the war; and a young frightened girl speaks out against the war.[1]

One of Bishop's major challenges during her tenure at the Library of Congress was to express her conflicted viewpoints. It is therefore not surprising that she relied so heavily upon a strategy of intertwined consent and dissent.

While the complexity of Bishop's life situation at this time should not be oversimplified by arguing that everything can be traced to her political anxieties, her positioning in early postwar politics has not been considered sufficiently. Bishop's medical record bore out a deep need to withdraw from the public position, even if we allow for the importance of her other longstanding physical and mental afflictions. It appears to be more than a matter of coincidence that Bishop spent so much of her time in withdrawal or on the sidelines in Yaddo and the Library of Congress, two of poetry's "hot spots" in this early Cold War, politically encumbered by anyone's analysis today.

Bishop's acute distress was compounded further by two other facts. Bishop was in a job for the first time in her life. In addition, she was a lesbian at a time of extraordinary surveillance of homosexual government employees, resulting in their branding as traitors of enemies of the state, their dismissal from jobs, and the ruin of their lives. This last fact especially has not been adequately considered in relation to her life and work in Washington.[2] The year's public silence cannot be taken at face value, then, as only the result, as Dickie and Millier have argued, of the fact that she did not respond as she had earlier to Paris architecture, or that the year provided many personal and medical problems (associated, for instance, with her alcoholism), but few "subjects for poems" (Dickie 112; Millier, *Elizabeth Bishop* 219-27).

Bishop responded very early in the fall of 1949 to Washington's nationalistic or patriotic cultural forms, including architecture, just as sensitively and intensively as she had to the Paris architecture during her interwar travels. The poem "Paris, 7 A.M.," related to her pre–World War II trip there, for example, meditates pointedly upon earlier Continental wars: "Where is the ammunition, the piled-up balls . . . ? (*CP* 26). So, too, Bishop searched the landscape in Washington for signs of war and victory culture during her 1949-50 appointment in Washington. But she found herself in a very different rhetorical environment. In Paris, she was the outside U.S. observer free of government rebuke. She did not enjoy this freedom in Cold War Washington.

We can see her predicament in a letter to the literary editor at *Harper's Bazaar* and a later editor at *The New Yorker,* Pearl Kazin Bell, whom she had met at Yaddo with Alfred Kazin. Bishop's response to Washington architecture seems written with an understanding that a second pair of hostile eyes might also read it to gather incriminating evidence, a realistic concern at this point with McCarthyism. Ames's secretary at Yaddo had spied on everyone. Marjorie Stevens was concerned during the Second World War about what she wrote in her letters to Bishop. Engelhardt reports that HUAC had a million dossiers of workers for security checks by 1949 (119). He also points out that offices were illegally entered and numerous burglaries committed. Unknown to themselves, millions of citizens gained a dossier self, a shadow persona. This was identity politics, 1950s style (119).

The result in a 1949 letter is a rhetoric that presents a confounded consent and dissent. Read one way, the letter sounds frivolously apolitical; read another, politically contentious. It reveals how treasonous Bishop would have sounded if she had expressed openly and without censorship her views in public and had published her commentary, not what one have expected from Bishop given the dominant image of her as silent and ill during this period. She deflates official Washington's power of ideological representation by deriding its architecture. Her use of the letter—a personal and private form of writing—suggests that she felt the need to articulate her disillusionment about the direction of postwar national culture dominated by the political right:

> Washington doesn't seem quite real. All those piles of granite and marble, like an inflated copy of *another* capital city someplace else (the Forum?). Even the Lincoln Memorial, which I went to see, affected me that way . . . . (*OA* 194)

Instead of viewing Washington's architecture as the stirring patriotic site of the unique savior-nation of the world in Cold War "containment" mythology, Bishop sees it first as merely "piles of granite and marble," drained of any inherent patriotic "romance" to stir the hearts of U.S. patriots. Her image of "piles of granite and marble" evokes cemetery markers, the deadly reality behind the bravado of Cold War militarism. Then she tosses the city with the unique "messianic" Cold War mission aside as an "inflated copy" of a "someplace else" that she cannot quite place. Even the Lincoln Memorial fails to stir her at a time when, as *Life* proclaimed in its January 2, 1950, blockbuster issue on the rise of the United States to its international superpower status, Lincoln was promoted as the greatest U.S. figure of the nineteenth century ("The Golden Years Before the Wars" 28). Such deflationary rhetoric exposing the nation's hubris seems unthinkable for a national poetry consultant in a victory culture interested in celebrating and revering itself.

While this reading is valid, Bishop's derision does not appear alone. It is highly muted in the actual context of the overall letter to Bell because Bishop's main discussion in the letter is aesthetics. She interlaces it with references to their recent stay in Yaddo so that the commentary seems apolitical—more of a conversation between two women about the arts. It appears that she is simply being an architecture critic.

In 1950 Bishop began keeping a diary, a largely overlooked handwritten diary of 1950 at the Vassar Archives, which records several of her events, experiences, and thoughts during this year, with many of the prose and poetry entries written in the same derogatory tone on topics similar to what we find in her letter to Bell. This journal holds the drafts of "View of the Capitol from the Library of Congress," the only published poem officially completed in 1950, revealing that she commented upon the Capitol building lengthily and muted her politically charged views in the published version of the poem. The poem also offers an example of Bishop's use of such crucial strategies of subversion as reporting on a specific cultural event—an air force band concert, creating a "readerly" poem; rewriting a part of her 1950 journal; multiply coding the poem; and relying upon strategic self-censorship and silence. Millier first drew attention to the existence of these poetry drafts but referred to them only under the title "Verdigris" (*Elizabeth Bishop* 224). Bishop transformed "Verdigris" into the published poem in her journal.[3]

This journal also contains notes about Pound, whom she visited as part of her job. They display the ambivalence informing her final published version of the poem "Visits to St. Elizabeths," written at least by early 1951 because Jarrell praised Bishop for it in a letter dated April 7, 1951 (Folder 5.9, VC). This poem parodies the nursery rhyme, "This is the house that Jack built," but also reports on a specific historical event—Pound's incarceration for treason. In addition, Bishop waited for a more open political moment to publish the poem as well as engaging in the subversive tactics of rewriting her journal, multiply coding the poem, and using self-censorship and silence about her visits during the year of national appointment.

In addition, the diary includes remarks about Bishop's private life and her female-centered circle, a risky rhetorical move given the era's conflation of Communism with homosexuality while she held public office and the government's penchant for the surveillance and private investigation of public employees (Bérubé and Edelman). "A Cold Spring" and some of her love poetry collected in the 1955 volume *A Cold Spring* are linked to journal entries. They also offer examples of self-censorship and silence as well as multiple coding.

Given the homophobic climate of the decade, it is astonishing that Bishop won a Pulitzer Prize in 1956 for a collection with so much lesbian-focused poetry. *A Cold Spring* appeared as the second section of the volume *Poems: North & South—A Cold Spring*, which Houghton Mifflin published in 1955, reprinting her first book. The volume contains poems written for Crane, Dewey, Holiday, Miller, Soares, and Stevens as well as "Four Poems," a highly erotic lesbian poetry sequence, "Roosters," and the poems about Europe from her travels with Crane and Miller.

The diary of 1950 by itself creates an informative "intertext" with "From Trollope's Journal," which was written during the 1950s and completed by the end of the decade. Several entries in her 1950 diary on official Washington contain a similar condescending outside observer's tone, so she perhaps recognized Trollope's usefulness to her as an alter ego. She took excerpts from Trollope's journal and arranged them to create her published poem just as she took quotations from her own journal of 1950 to create some of her other poetry. She draws attention in the poem, then, to her own corresponding poetic method of extricating passages from a journal and transforming them into poetry. This strategy is highlighted in her decision to title the poem "From Trollope's Journal" rather than, for example, "Trollope Looks at Washington," suggesting that the reader consider the relevance of the journal with the poem.

In addition to providing Bishop with a Civil War history for criticizing the Cold War victory culture, Trollope's journal also offered a way for her to allegorize her personal Cold War narrative in her professional and private lives. The poem offers yet another example of Bishop's reliance upon multiple subversion strategies: waiting for an open moment of publication, using multiple codes, and employing self-censorship and silence.

"View of the Capitol from the Library of Congress" contains both Bishop's ideological critique of militarization and her equally important concern about military domination of the home front and private citizens. More specifically, she sharply denounces national Cold War support for air warfare in the Korean War. This reading agenda seems weighty for a poem that has generally been dismissed as simply an amusing anecdote on the ways that the trees block the sound of the air force band playing at the Capitol—its most visible and reader-accessible text too frivolous for serious consideration. Indeed it has been generally overlooked in published Bishop scholarship.

Bishop's playfulness in the poem possesses a "fairy tale" tone that presents a kind of heightened "romantic" response to the air force band music. The childlike voice that admired Nova Scotian soldiers in the Great War and the "raging heroism" of the roosters in World War II's "Roosters" asserts itself here, apparently mesmerized by the theatrics or spectacle of the scene. The music, for instance, is seen as "gold-dust," with each "big leaf" sagging under the weight of it. Indeed in a first scanning, one might interpret the poem as one listener's Penelope-like enthralled rapture with the patriotic music attempting to woo citizens into war support and national solidarity. At first glance, then, its speaker appears visibly complicitous with Cold War expectations for the nation's citizens:

> I think the trees must intervene,
>
> catching the music in their leaves
> like gold-dust, till each big leaf sags.
>
> . . . .
>
> Great shades, edge over,
> give the music room.
> The gathered brasses want to go
> *boom—boom.* (*CP* 69)

But as one begins to reread the text, one realizes that Bishop finds the trees, not the band, magical. The childlike tone serves to underscore the vulnerability of a revered pastoral world of innocence left as a potentially helpless victim against the "boom—boom" of the air force. This tone functions much like the imagery of children at play in "V-Day August 14th, 1945."

The national patriotic music cannot be heard clearly. So its courting or persuasion among citizen-listeners falters. Millier's and Dickie's recent assessments that the published poem represents Bishop's skeptical perspective on military life are also quite correct, then.[4] As Dickie argues, Bishop seems to criticize the air force band's "feeble" efforts to "declare its own glory or even assert its military presence" (Millier 223; Dickie 112-13).

Bishop's correspondence during her 1949-50 year in Washington, D.C., with her good friends MacIver and Frankenberg support this second, antimilitarist readings of the poem as a whole in addition to the more apolitical reading favored for so long. She enclosed the final poem in a letter dated only as Sunday morning in October 1950 while she was at Yaddo following her poetry position (*OA* 210). Bishop had agreed to send them postcards of the Washington sights/sites while she worked as poetry chair and hoped the poem would suffice as a substitute for a card with a view, joining the cards that she had sent depicting the Washington Monument, the cherry trees, and other national sightseeing spots.[5]

Bishop's preoccupation with the patriotic and political sights/sites of the national capitol during 1949-50 documented in correspondence to Bell, MacIver, and Frankenberg also indicates her intense scrutiny of the city from her writing desk. She described Washington to Frankenberg in a letter dated August 21, 1950, several weeks after the U.S. troops arrived in Korea and near the anniversary of the bombing of Japan, as though it had been invaded and overtaken by the military. An air force base seems to have suddenly sprung up and obliterated the spring landscape. Indeed her depiction recalls her World War II–era letters to Russell and Moore describing airplanes in the spring and the arrival of the navy. Her description to Frankenberg during the Korean War masculinizes the metallic apparatus of militarism and suggests the feminization of nature more explicitly through her depiction of spring as beautiful, but also fragile:

> Washington seems composed of equal parts of airplanes, starings, electric drills, and thick, oily storm. The beautiful spring lasted exactly one week. (August 21, 1950, Folder 29.9 VC)

Bishop's journal of 1950, however, complicates this double or binary reading of the published poem as visible compliance intertwined with quasi-visible dissent. It draws attention to the way that Bishop interlaces these two strategies with a quasi-(in)visible unacceptable dissent and silence about her private life in the poem's drafts and fragments. The private prose narrative interrupts the poetry and offers digression as well as crucial context for the poetry drafts.

Bishop signals the importance of her private life in relation to the poem by writing in prose across the front of the journal that 1950 was her "worst year" so far (Folder 77.4, VC). She then begins the poem on the page dated Friday, January 13, 1950, but noted at the bottom that the date was actually January 26. With her hospital stay over Christmas, the intrusive experience of an interview for *The Boston Post* news story in early January on her work as poetry consultant, and her basic dislike of the Washington job, she found herself staving off depression.

She recorded in this first prose entry her fascination with the mossy facade of the U.S. post office building in a childlike voice of awe that one can hear in the published version of the poem and in the depiction of the heroic roosters in "Roosters." It offers a contrasting juxtaposition to the voice of despair about the problematical year of 1950: "How wonderful this place would look if all the facades were like this" (Folder 77.4, p.3, VC).

A few lines later, however, Bishop switched abruptly from prose to

poetry and outlined the beginning of the poem. Among the lines is a critique of justice in the Capitol through her use of stiff and harsh moss
imagery. Combining physical observation with political commentary in
this image, Bishop depicts justice with an implied eroticized deadly masculinization of feminized nature that foreshadows her eventual letter to
Frankenberg describing the military occupation of Washington, D.C.
(Folder 77.4, p.3, VC).

While one can begin to discern the intertwined voices of awe and sharp
denunciation already forming in the poem, the journal reveals yet another
dimension to the vacillation between the exuberant "how wonderful . . ."
phrase and the image of stiff harsh moss. Between these two observations,
Bishop jots down, "Louise Crane just called—I'm seeing her tomorrow." This
brief, apparently unrelated interjection on Bishop's private life reminds the
reader that lesbian life was under the surveillance of the government with little justice to be expected. It therefore helps account for the contrasting tones
of awe and dejection both because of the public politics and likely private
conflict. It is unclear just how involved Bishop was at this time with Crane,
although they remained lifelong friends. It reveals as well the importance of
the silenced lifetext in the journal for informing and adding complexity to
the dissent in the poem, providing a quasi-(in)visible layering within it.

On the next journal page apparently also written on January 26, Bishop
continued her strategy of combining physical observation with political
commentary and sketched out an unexpectedly biting satire in prose. She
noted that the "flying flags" in Washington seemed like "horny insects,"
another masculinization of the nation's most patriotic symbol (Folder 77.4,
p. 4, VC). Then she added in prose on the same page:

> The light moves from left to far left & off
> around on the
> lighted tier of little windows on the Capitol dome . . .
> giving an effect of a big old wall-eyed white horse

Her depiction of the light illuminated on the Capitol dome suggests
that the Capitol, the architectural symbol of U.S. national government
because it houses the Congress, seems awry. The light reminds her of a "big
old wall-eyed white horse," with one eye that squints to the side rather than
straight ahead. Here the problem seems to be that the Capitol light can
move only "left to far left," intimating that the Capitol has limited vision. Is
this just a physical observation by Bishop, or a political observation? Given
her earlier comment about the "harsh, stiff Justice on the Dome," as well as

her interjected note about Crane, one is tempted to read this as a very well-camouflaged comment upon the HUAC hearings and Senator Joseph McCarthy's probes at this time that attacked many private citizens, especially targeting homosexuals, liberals, intellectuals, and cultural producers as a whole (see Bérubé and Edelman). Moreover, the "white horse" here is not the heroic horse one expects to see depicted, but a horse with abnormal vision veering off course as it fixates on the "left to far left."

While the images of the light, Capitol dome, and horse became part of the published version of the poem, the most caustic prose statement about this military-dominated Washington, D.C. in this fragmented piece of writing did not. Still writing in prose, Bishop indicated with the notation "Washington poem" that she was beginning to think of these random prose notes an images as a basis for a poem. Then, in a strong, direct sexual language atypical of her, Bishop personified the national Capitol dome as the food source for the military. The dome, it seems to me, functions as a kind of Cold War Penelope figure, the "good feminine woman," following Friedan's analysis of the new binary good/evil "Cold War" American woman—the mother/femme fatale. Bishop calls the dome "an elaborate sugar-tit for a nation that likes sugar." Moreover, the "airplanes" settle themselves gingerly "down" so near the "Dome" in her prose that it looks like the airplanes are trying to land on the "sugar-tit." The image suggested here by the airplanes with their wings is of bees—after their nectar or sugar from the dome, the metaphorical flower with the petals down and "tit" exposed in full view.

Is this a fanciful observation by Bishop, or political commentary? When one considers that the military draws its "sugar" or "food source" from congressional financial appropriations, it is difficult to see this as mere whimsical imagery. The Congress represented by the Capitol dome functions not only as the Cold War "good woman" who remains faithful and welcomes home her troops wholeheartedly, but also as the "good faithful patriotic mother" who nourishes her military forces and supports military "occupations" abroad and at home. Indeed the Pentagon budget more than quadrupled between 1948 and 1953, from $10.9 billion to $49.6 billion, laying the base of "militarized prosperity" and the military-industrial government complex (Engelhardt 75):

> (Washington airplanes always setting themselves gingerly poem)
>   down
>   Dome — also an elaborate sugar-tit for a
> nation
> that likes sugar (Folder 77.4, p. 4, VC)

Bishop's Feb. 4 prose entry on the January 27, 1950 page indicates her desire to remove the flag, the nation's major patriotic symbol, from the scene altogether: ". . . . put the flags away . . . pull down the flags" (Folder 77.4, p. 5, VC).

On February 21, just after she had declined to read at the New York YMHA, she reinserted the vexing flags, which remained permanently in the poem, conveying a meaning similar to that of the "sugar-tit" (Folder 77.4, p. 12, VC). While discarding this specific passage in her development of the poem, Bishop retained her denunciation of the nation's "feeding" of the military in the published poem's lines: "Unceasingly the little flags / feed their limp stripes into the air" (*CP* 69). The red and white stripes remind one of candy canes being fed into the air, where air force planes come and go. But this specific batch of candy seems repellant: "impotent" with "little" flags feeding "limp" stripes.

Bishop's decision to deflate the flag's power is signaled in her March 31 entry, shortly after McCarthy's intensive new drive on Communism, on the February 23 page, where she was still preoccupied with the flags. With March winds, she wrote, "flags going at higher speed." She then critiqued their use on holidays as decorative, even frivolous:

> On Washington's Birthday the trolley-cars had 2 small flags stuck on either side of the front, on top—they fly them on most holidays. The flags are very small and the effect is rather silly, "cute." (Folder 77.4, p. 14, VC)

This strong judgment on the flags also seems related to one of her visits to Pound. She wrote about him on February 23, sandwiched between her discussion about the irritating flags and her condemnation of the use of flags on national patriotic holidays as "silly." This juxtaposition indicates that Pound figures in previously unrecognized ways in "View of the Capitol from the Library of Congress."

In her diary entry, Bishop reveals in prose her ambivalence about her visits to Pound which were required in the job:

> Took Weldon Kees to St Elizabeths with me to call on Pound—I think I left my favorite pen there—we didn't get there until almost 3:30 because I had completely forgotten (the perfect slip) that visiting hours were one to four. He was very talkative—has a new blue black chair; already broken from his throwing himself back in it, almost full-length. He said he was using my hair-lotion—I think it was eau-de-cologne, though. (Folder 77.4, p. 13, VC)

Several months later, after the high point of her year at the Dylan Thomas reading and the low point with Jarrell, she returned to the notebook. In an entry on the June 23 page with the notation of the location in Washington, Bishop began working again on the eventual poem but using prose. She added in the band, describing it as "unreal" as the architecture she had deplored to Bell in an earlier letter. Her image of the band with its "short burst" and "vol. or volume/volley" links music to gunfire and cannon volley in war, for patriotic music is used both to mobilize and direct soldiers against the enemy and to mask the horrifying sounds of actual warfare:

> The band playing on the steps of the Capitol—it sounds unreal, a sort of *imagined* band, in short burst, vol. There isn't any wind, and looking out one has the sensation that this effect is being caused by the great masses of the trees between the band and here. (Folder 77.4, p. 16, VC)

The all-important juxtaposition of the visual and the aural in this poem that I will take up later emphasizes the fact that the poem's speaker appears both visibly compliant by appearing to listen yet resistant because she does not hear the sound. In fact the published version highlights this startling incongruity with the use of the word "queer." The journal page on the same date as the above entry fills in the larger picture behind Bishop's barest hint in her poem about her sexuality. Immediately following the imagined "short burst" of the band music is an unusual emotional outburst from Bishop:

> I think when one is extremely unhappy—almost hysterically unhappy, that is—it is one's time to lie down. All that long stretch—several years ago—it wasn't just a matter of not being able to accept the present, that present, although it began that way possibly. But the past and the present seemed confused or contradicting each other violently and constantly, and the past wouldn't "lie down."

After this emotional confession or purging, Bishop reveals that she has found a way to calm the storm: "Going to Jane D's this afternoon, thank goodness." She spent much of her time relaxing at Dewey's Maryland home while in Washington and inscribed her poem "A Cold Spring" in the 1955 volume *A Cold Spring*, "for Jane Dewey, Maryland" (*CP* 55).

Dewey's farm Havre de Grace offered Bishop a pastoral setting. But Dewey was in charge of terminal ballistics at Aberdeen, fifteen miles from her home, and when Bishop stayed there writing she told Lowell that the ground would shake from Dewey's tests at the proving ground with a boom (*OA* 204-205). So the ballistics testing kept the Cold War in Bishop's mind during her year in Washington just as the navy had reminded her continually of World War II in Key West.

Bishop's complex June 24 and June 25 entry with a notation about her location in Maryland at Dewey's records the poem's title and sketches out the poem for the first time. It reveals that she will combine her derisive views of the patriotic architecture with those of the patriotic music played by the military band. Patriotic or nationalistic music is supposed to achieve its wooing of its citizens through group identification with the music, not brute force; but Bishop sees the band's desire to coerce fully with its "boom-boom" warlike sound.

The "Maryland" notation places the poet in a sympathetic (although illegal by the terms of Cold War culture) female-centered landscape away from the confines of official Washington and therefore accords her a measure of security and distance to view the national capital and its victory culture. It is not surprising, given this, that Bishop foregrounds struggle between the trees (citizenry and home front) and the music (military and government) with her use of double columns, a device that also organizes the highly regarded Vietnam-era antimilitarist poem "12 O'Clock News" as well as one of its 1950 versions—"Desk at Night" (Folder 77.4, p. 16, VC).

On June 25 she recorded a final fragment of the poem-in-progress in double columns. It continues to focus on the music, which wants to exert its military strength in warlike sounds, indicating that the trees block and overpower it. The reference to the fact that music both must do this as well as wants to do it gives it a masculine and highly sexually charged edge, to which the feminized "trees," or the nation's citizens as well as other nations, are commanded to yield. The parallel between this masculine/feminine binary in these fragments and the published poem and the Cold War militarism's domination of the private feminized citizen sphere (heterosexual as well as lesbian) is uncanny (Folder 77.4, p. 17, VC).

While these tensions can be read from the published poem, Bishop's journal of 1950 offers a quasi-(in)visible layering of dissent. In both sets of double columns in the poem's drafts, the music from the right column appears to invade and dominate the left column representing the trees. In each version the music's need "to go boom" ends the poem, offering an unresolved conflict between the two opposing forces.

But the "boom" of the military music intensifies in the second draft's set of columns. What has occurred between the first draft and second of the two-column poem is Bishop's description of a party for antiwar writer John Dos Passos concluded by a thunderstorm that seems to infiltrate the landscape of "View of the Capitol from the Library of Congress," with its own booming sound. Bishop writes in her 1950 journal about a "grey twilight filled with fireflies. I've never so many. . . . In the light they looked greenish."

Bishop uses fireflies in the poem publicly meant for Dewey, "A Cold Spring." She also uses imagery from this journal entry in her four love poems entitled "Four Poems." In "II/Rain Towards Morning," she describes a wire crashing down in the rain freeing a million birds (*CP* 77). Then in "III/While Someone Telephones," she writes of two lost fireflies (*CP* 78). Finally, in "IV/O Breath," she relies heavily upon the image of flying (*CP* 79).

It is significant that Bishop interweaves discourse about her personal life with the poem's drafts. Through the journal, she was able to inscribe her publicly silenced subjectivity as a lesbian into her dialogue with the nation's Cold War "containment" culture. She was not able to narrate her story easily, however. In fact, one is struck by how spasmodic both the prose and poetry entries are, as well as how rare. Although this journal's struggles can be read persuasively by following Lombardi's concerns in *The Body & The Song* about Bishop's illnesses (i.e., the asthmatic's struggle for breath) and restrictive sexual positioning, its primary tie to the suffocating politics of Washington must not be underestimated.

The journal in fact seems to offer another example in Bishop's writing of the fragmentation of language or cultural representation in the face of silencing and subsequent attempts to break the silence with speech. In addition, it reads in such fragments that one wonders if she was concerned with detection and exposure within her private diary space. The fragments could not be read to incriminate her readily. In some respects the journal's "music" is like the band's in the published poem: "it comes in snatches, dim then keen, / then mute, and yet there is no breeze" (*CP* 69).

While the subject position of the journal writer is identified readily as female and indirectly as lesbian by those who know about Bishop's biography, the published poem's speaker bears nonspecific or universal social markings, an apparent visible compliance by Bishop with dominant Cold War culture's denial of social differentiation (see May). Yet the reader of the poem tends to refer to the poem's speaker as female. The reader may be drawn into this problematical identification by conflating the speaker's gender and sexual coding with the poet's or coding the poem's language ("one small lunette," "gold-dust," "little flags," and "great shades") as feminine, following traditional midcentury views of language explicated by such linguistics scholars as Robin Lakoff, who has described this kind of language as "talking like a lady" (280-91).

Camouflaged lesbian concerns are present as well in the poem. In the final published poem the speaker listens to impotent patriotic music that "doesn't quite come through" in spite of being played "hard and loud" by an all-male air force band:

> the Air Force Band
> in uniforms of Air Force blue
> is playing hard and loud (*CP* 69)

Apparently the sound does not carry because the feminized landscape of "the giant trees stand in between" and "must intervene" by "catching the music in their leaves . . . till each big leaf sags" (69). In contrast to the power of the trees to absorb the weight of the music, the "little flags / feed their limp stripes into the air, / and the band's efforts vanish there" (69). Because "the gathered brasses want to go/ *boom—boom,*" a reference to the military commanders or "brasses" who want to go to war as well as a caustic comment on the infantilism of war in the use of "boom—boom," the speaker urges the "great shades" to "edge over" and "give the music room," a physical impossibility.

Equally important, the speaker says that it's "queer," that the music does not come through. Moreover, the word "queer" flanked on two sides by dashes—the only instance in the poem—appears visually in stanza two to block the music.[6] Given the Cold War ostracism of lesbianism from the "body politic," it is not surprising that the poem's speaker has difficulty hearing the patriotic music designed to "court" her citizen loyalty.

The military music—like the Fascist roosters in "Roosters"—is intent on "capturing" its own citizens. Under the guise of "courting" patriotic music is the harsh reality that the "brasses want to go *boom—boom*" into the citizen crowd. In other words, the patriotic music camouflages a kind of warfare against citizens. The patriotic wooing is clearly rebuffed—or resisted—by the private citizen speaker-listener in the poem as well as by the trees representing the feminized civilian or private sphere of the nation.

What makes this poem an even more forceful antimilitarist statement about the dangers of the nation's "courting" of its citizens is the juxtaposition of the visual discourse against the aural discourse. What one sees is not what one hears, for the listener can see the band playing but not hear the music clearly. At this point the poem's conflicted visual and aural discourses produce heterogeneous meanings that are not easily resolved and restabilized. For example, this conflict seems an apt cultural representation of the citizen-listener who ostensibly listens to the patriotic music and thus conforms to the image of a patriotic citizen. Simultaneously, however, citizen resistance is intimated as the music fails to penetrate the ear and thus to enter into the citizen's body.

From another angle, this juxtaposition highlights the duplicity in Cold War militarism's patriotic music. The music camouflages and sanitizes the unseen grim reality of war and suffering—perhaps the use of air warfare that Bishop more openly attacks in her journal drafts. The double columns of trees and music in earlier drafts are merged and locked into unresolved conflict within the apparently smooth-running stanzas of the published poem. The result is a poem with two antagonistic discursive surfaces: the first, a gliding linear surface if one goes with the published version; the second, a combative jagged merger of two competing columns if one works from the journal drafts into the final published poem. In the final published version, Bishop suppresses her own perception of conflict and submerges it beneath the polished surface of the poem.

Both the drafts and notes in the journal as well as the published poem hardly offer a sentimental, appreciative evocation of a year as poetry consultant to the Library of Congress. The national capitol—with such nationalistic cultural forms as patriotic music—seems askew, unable to inspire an eroticized "love of country" or national allegiance as it did with Wayne, discussed earlier in the book. But this does not mean that the poet or the eyewitness-storyteller in the poem has escaped the reach of nationalistic fervor altogether.

The eyewitness-observer does appear to be complicit because he or she does not leave the scene or engage in a more open disengagement process. Indeed, he or she urges the trees to move over for the music. The poet, moreover, undermines the credibility of the eyewitness-observer because the trees obviously cannot physically move over independently and yet he or she seems to think that they can. This destabilization calls into question the rest of the views in the poem: i.e., is there really a problem with the horse? So it would seem that with every dissenting move, a countermove camouflages or confounds it. The horse's blindness, the eyewitness-storyteller's questionable vision, the poet's closeted position of dissent within visible compliance—all three draw attention to the larger framework of skewered vision.

In any case, Bishop's poem does not support a reading of Cold War Washington as the center of an exalted, extraordinary nation that should permit even harmful behavior for a higher good. The air force music does not justify an invasion of the landscape and removal of the trees, one of the effects of warfare.

Bishop's poem is prescient, forewarning that this Cold War narrative would fail even at this early stage in Korea. In a parallel response within popular culture, the war comic books had moved from the patriotic nationalism of World War II to ambiguity and ambivalence about the Korean War (Hilbish 210).

Bishop's attempts to resist the invasiveness of patriotic courting as a cultural producer while appearing to accommodate it reveals a rhetorical and real strategy for dealing with Cold War cultural surveillance. Bishop already knew that her poetry office at the Library of Congress was under siege. The awarding of the Bollingen Prize to Pound had created an uproar that continued at a high level throughout her fall in office.

So Bishop's relationship to Pound was complex. She found Pound objectionable. She was worried about him in the late summer and early fall. Pfeiffer's letter of September 23, 1949, indicates that Bishop was considering living with a black family in Washington, where segregation was still very predominant. Pfeiffer told Bishop that her plan would help poetry and remove a "Pound" of odor from poetry (Folder 17.10, VC). Then in her letter of October 10, 1949, Pfeiffer urged Bishop to declare the Pound matter closed (Folder 17.10, VC). According to Kees who visited him with her, she did not "care much for Pound, regarding him as a pretty dangerous character, through his influence—particularly the anti-Semitism—on the young" (Fountain 14).

Ironically Pound represented the quintessential patriotic poet who used his art to promote a nationalist military state. The fact that he espoused the cause of a U.S. enemy placed him in a complex relation to the whole question of the relationship between nationalist ideology and cultural production. His incarceration or "containment" in St. Elizabeth's Hospital for his public treason rather than death, because he was deemed mentally unstable, cast him as an alien, diseased "other" outside of the new definition of U.S. citizenship. Yet the right-wing-dominated national Cold War ideology demanded that the nation's poets imitate Pound in his unswerving loyalty to a nationalist belief system and thus embrace his "disease" and state of "house arrest" or "containment" for the sake of national security and patriotism.

In either victory culture plot, the poet risked living metaphorically as Pound did: "in a room with no doors, . . . no privacy. . . . People would go in and out, guards and other patients . . ." (Fountain 114–15).

It is not surprising, then, that Pound is intertwined with Bishop's drafting of the poem "View of the Capitol from the Library of Congress." He figured in her daily life and job too prominently. He was, after all, the "military music" that she wished to resist. Moreover, one could say that his incarceration and the removal of his poetry prize placed her metaphorically, as well as the position itself, under a version of "house arrest,": "in a room with . . . no privacy."

Bishop's complex treatment of Pound as the representative patriotic poet reveals her ambivalent attitude toward this political predicament of the poet in the Cold War "historical moment." Her decision to cast the published poem "Visits to St. Elizabeths" that she later wrote underscores anxieties about the eventual outcome of political pressures on poetry and poets. Bishop characterizes Pound as a "tragic, talkative, honored, old, brave, cranky, cruel, busy, tedious, wretched" man "that lies in the house of Bedlam" as she writes him into twelve stanzas of rhyme (*CP* 133–35).[7] The poem's horrifying message is brought out by the startling juxtaposition between a child's song, not unlike the lullaby in "Songs for a Colored Singer" with its accompanying associations of innocence, and the images of incomprehensible World War II human suffering and cruelty.

While the poem's subject is obviously Pound from the title and the year 1950, Bishop creates a distance between the autobiographical connection to Pound and "the man that lies in the house of Bedlam" by never naming Pound directly in the poem. One must go from written text to life text to the private journal of 1950, then, to interpret the poem fully. This enables one to see the complex entanglements among Bishop, Pound, and national politics. She focuses solely on him as a "man," except in the eleventh stanza where she describes him as "the poet, the man" (*CP* 135). As a man she finds him a fractured subject—wretched, brave, old, cruel—caught up in a state of "infantile arrest" and frozen in time.

Dickie and Millier have argued that her visits to him "were also a confrontation with her own weakness and guilt, . . . succumbing to bouts of alcoholism . . ." (Dickie 13; Millier 220–22). Then, too, they write, she could weigh out probable similarities between his mental and emotional state and her mother's much earlier nervous breakdown and hospitalization as well as her own.

What remains fully unacknowledged, however, is her homosexuality while the Cold War was pathologizing it as sickness, treason, and Communism. In even her private journal, she engaged in what Catherine Stimpson calls the "lesbian lie," a pretense that no lesbian exists where in fact she does (152-66).

Did she feel, then, that her life was similar to Pound's? I do not think so. As the earlier journal entry reveals, she tried to escape him—she had "forgotten (the perfect slip)" about the visiting hours for Pound and took Kees there for only the last thirty minutes of the allowed visitation period. Moreover, as Dickie has correctly argued, she passes judgment on his horrific role in the war very memorably in the final stanza of the poem (113):

> This is the soldier home from the war.
> These are the years and the walls and the door
> that shut on a boy that pats the floor
> to see if the world is round or flat.
> This is a Jew in a newspaper hat
> that dances carefully down the ward,
> walking the plank of a coffin board
> with the crazy sailor
> that shows his watch
> that tells the time
> of the wretched man
> that lies in the house of Bedlam. (*CP* 135)

The poem is not only about Pound, but about any poet collaborating with a military state—exactly her own possible predicament as a government employee in a right-wing militarized 1949-50 Washington demanding patriotic nationalism of its employees. In Bishop's view, poetry's support of such violence and devastation in World War II, as Dickie argues, referring to Bishop's line in stanza nine, "this is a world of books gone flat," undermines the assumed moral value of poetry in such a world (113). As Bishop indicates in "V-Day August 14th, 1945" the world had gone flat, blasted into tiny fragments.

Given her personal and professional anxieties about military culture and its domination of the home front and private citizens, it is not unexpected that Bishop's final stanza memorializes the sufferings of war rather than the heroics. This is the strategy of her archival fragment about V-Day. Rather than a heroic soldier in the poem based on Pound, we find the plain observation that "this is the soldier home from the war," directing one to consider as well the soldiers who did not come home. Then, the boy is shown as one of war's victims. He is shut in by the world it has left and must test out its instability as now both a round and flat devastated shape. Next, the victimized Jew is shown "walking the plank of a coffin board," his suffering marked earlier in previous stanzas through his weeping and widowerhood. The "crazy" sailor obsessed with time has lost his mind to the war. All these lives were at the mercy of the "time" of the "watch," the poetic measure of music "of the wretched man that lies," collaborating with the Fascist militarism that destroyed them.

As Bishop wrote in her journal of 1950, then, she was accumulating a long list of grievances to indict militarism for poisoning "the air" of her poetic and private worlds in "From Trollope's Journal." But even during the more "open" political moment of the late 1950s and early 1960s, she chose the path of obliqueness rather than directness in the poem. The self-protective "version" of Bishop was obviously still editing her more political "versions" that sought a significant dialogue with the Cold War national narrative just as it had attempted a more sustained conversation with the World War II narrative.

"From Trollope's Journal" offers a retrospective on the year in Washington with intertwined visible, quasi-visible, quasi-(in)visible, and silenced multitexts. Bishop's intertext with Anthony Trollope's Civil War–era journal in the poem is self-evident from the poem's title. Through her appropriation of his journal in the poem, Bishop treats Trollope's negative rendering of the crucial Civil War "founding" scene of U.S. federalism's dominance in the United States. Interestingly, she decided to shape the poem as a sonnet, a Western poetic form long associated with conquest and political struggle as well as courtly love and chivalric culture and more heavily politicized by New Historicist critics beginning with Stephen Greenblatt and Louis Montrose. To be exact, as Goldensohn has pointed out, Bishop wrote the poem as a double sonnet (236–37). Lowell, however, suggested that she drop the double sonnet division and create one long stanza of dramatic monologue in a letter dated July 12, 1960 (*OA* 420).

Bishop presents a Trollope primarily interested in the military state of President Abraham Lincoln's Civil War Washington. Yet it is clear that Trollope saw this national historical "moment" grounded in the nation's earlier "founding" moment as a separate nation under the first U.S. President, the U.S. military commander in the American Revolution, General George Washington. Bishop quotes Trollope's observations on the Native American statuary depicting Washington's "foster sons," thereby highlighting the nation's roots in militarism and racism.

Depicting Trollope's views of the "White House" as a large farm with a barnyard commandeered and transformed into a bloody battle site not unlike the setting of her own World War II–era Key West home and her poem "Roosters," Bishop presents the ravages, and not the glories, of the U.S. Civil War. Indeed, one is reminded that more than the Second World War is such a battle site for Bishop—the Great War, the Korean War, and the Cold War also must be considered.

According to Trollope in the poem, for example, the U.S. federal capital is built in a "sad, unhealthy" pastoral "swampy" spot occupied by the federal troops. Moreover, Trollope sees the U. S. "White House" as a barnyard of sickness and slaughter, whether because of the oxen and cattle, who provide food and transport for the troops, or the soldiers themselves, who are held in the pen until slaughter time on the battleground. The "ugly mud" is filled with "herds of cattle with legs caked the color of dried blood."

Trollope hardly offers a heroic portrayal of a "founding moment" in a nation's history. Indeed a discourse or language of pathology runs through out the poem, as the conclusion aptly illustrates:

> —they say the present President has got
> ague or fever in each backwoods limb. . . . .
> > Th'effluvium
> made that damned anthrax on my forehead throb.
> I called a surgeon in, a young man, but
> with a sore throat himself, he did his job.
> We talked about the War, and as he cut
> away, he croaked out, "Sir, I do declare
> everyone's sick! The soldiers poison the air." (*CP* 132)

So where does Trollope's view end and Bishop's begin? Bishop's appropriation of Trollope's journal is highly vexed, raising questions about who is actually speaking in the poem. Is it Bishop through Trollope? Trollope through Bishop? Are the voices so intermingled that they cannot be distinguished? As Bishop asks in "Poem," which addresses the art of place and memory in Nova Scotia, "which is which"?

One way to begin answering this question is to compare Trollope's journal with Bishop's poem. Bishop's remarkable ability to construct poetry out of a journal's prose through omission and distillation is apparent in this example of her development of the conclusion to "From Trollope's Journal." As indicated previously, the last six and a half lines of the poem focus on Trollope's encounter with a surgeon who treats a lesion on his forehead and remarks that the "soldiers poison the air." Trollope's journal offers this description:

> . . . . I was hardly out of the doctor's hands while I was there, and he did not support my theory as to the goodness of the air. "It is poisoned by the soldiers," he said, "and everybody is ill." But then my doctor was, perhaps, a little tinged with Southern proclivities. (21)

In an undated draft of her poem entitled "Trollope Looks at Washington," which is partially crossed out and revised to "Trollope In Washington," Bishop extrapolates the following from Trollope's prose excerpt:

> He has an anthrax on his forehead. The air "It is poisoned by the soldiers," he said (doctor) and everybody is ill." (Folder 49.1, VC)

By omitting Trollope's complicating consideration of the physician's questionable loyalties to the Union, Bishop is able to foreground the militaristic poisoning of the air. The surgeon's illness is attributed directly to the military scene in Washington, D.C. itself.

Bishop later admitted that the poem was really all Trollope's words, although she did not mention how sharply she had edited and reshaped it, and called it her "anti-Eisenhower" poem in a letter dated November 18, 1965, to Lowell (*OA* 252). This letter is crucial for tracing the intertextuality originating in "From Trollope's Journal," pointing us in two closely related directions. It refers us to Trollope's journal and points to the second important intertext for this poem: Bishop's covert Cold War intertext intertwined with her Civil War intertext with Trollope. This Cold War intertextuality begins in but extends beyond "From Trollope's Journal" to encompass Bishop's own journal of 1950.

Let's begin with why Bishop's revelation about the fugitive Cold War subtext in the poem appears in a letter so much later after her year as poetry consultant in Cold War Washington. As Dickie has perceptively written, the U.S. government might have considered the poem suspiciously anti-American or even treasonous if it had been published during the 1950s (114). More specifically, readers might have viewed Bishop's linkage of the Civil War and the Cold War through allegory as condemnation of the military-driven Presidency of the war hero Eisenhower. At least this offers one plausible interpretation. Given White's editorial decision at *The New Yorker* to hold up the poem's publication until after the U.S. election of

President John Kennedy in 1960, one cannot underestimate the role of national politics for poets in general throughout the 1950s and long after Bishop's tenure at the Library of Congress in Washington (*OA* 251). Indeed, in a September 14, 1960, letter to Bell, Bishop told her that her magazine had turned down the poem and she thought they felt she was critical of Eisenhower and admitted that this was true (Folder 24.10, VC).

While Bishop's revelation to Bell permits readers to draw a connection between the Civil War and Cold War in one brief global glance at "From Trollope's Journal," closer attention to the poem reveals even finer unread intertexts. The rhetoric of disease discussed earlier that runs throughout the poem and reaches a climax in the last two lines ("Sir, I do declare everyone's sick / the soldiers poison the air") offers a good example of how Bishop appropriates Trollope's words more specifically to serve her goal of creating a Cold War intertext with his Civil War text. This discourse of pathology suggests a Bishop dialogue with the Cold War discourse of "contamination." Countless examples of the discourse of "contamination" from the political right filled the media. They included the well-known cliché-ridden characterizations of Communism as an "epidemic" from FBI Director Hoover, or of Communists as "rats" by Vice-President Nixon (see, for example, such documentaries as *Seeing Red: Stories of American Communists*). Unlike the U.S. federal government, however, Bishop does not attribute the contamination or disease "inside" the nation's politics to a foreign or Communist source. She finds it rooted within the nation's military—the nation's soldiers "poison the air."

Sitting at the center of this Cold War capital, this national Cold War victory culture narrative, promising peace through "containment" was a military-managed presidency run by the Pentagon after 1945, or more specifically, President Eisenhower, whose presidency consolidated the nuclear military-industrial government complex. While he dressed in civilian clothes after the war, the historical visual image of Eisenhower in his general's uniform dominated the world's vision of him and the U.S. nation. As president from 1952 to 1960, he signaled to the world that the same general who had engineered the Allies into victory in World War II now led the U.S.-dominated Cold War "free world." The global image of the Cold War United States, then, coincided with the image of General-President Eisenhower, who held the trust of the Allies now interested in having the U.S. safeguard its interests in all respects—from the military to the cultural. In short, he represented the epitome of the national World War II–Cold War culture. Historian Jill Ker Conway offers an example of this dominant image abroad in her memoir account of her arrival in the United States in 1960 from her native Australia:

> Eisenhower, to me still a hero from the 1939-1945 war, was a villain to [the graduate student in history at Columbia]. Her eyes flashed as she told me how Ike had catered shamelessly to the red-baiting Senator Joseph McCarthy, and how he had presided over the buildup of the defense industry. (4-5)

In "From Trollope's Journal," Bishop seems to suggest through Trollope's words that Eisenhower, like the militaristic roosters in her own World War II "Roosters," belongs to a national history of militaristic violence, deceit, and dishonor that includes Washington and Lincoln. Why, for instance, are the statues of Native Americans, who represent the racially coded national conquest story, a "whitewashed stubby lot" and "foster sons" in the poem? Why only the allusive presence of African Americans in Civil War Washington? Why the troubling political inference that the peace and freedom enjoyed by a few is intertwined with violence against subjugated peoples at the nation's founding moment, the Civil War, and Cold War?

Finally, why the placement of the poem in Bishop's collection *Questions of Travel* just before "Visits to St. Elizabeths," indeed opposite this poem in *The Complete Poems,* a poem also dated inside parentheses—(1950)? Bishop's politics resists easy interpretation. Is she commenting upon Ezra Pound's controversial incarceration for treason in World War II at St. Elizabeth's during her tenure at the Library of Congress? Or does she wish to suggest that the Cold War year "1950" can be explained by a poem dated 1861, thereby analyzing the nation's Cold War political sickness as an outgrowth of its diseased history? Or are both readings valid?

Bishop does indeed suggest a relationship between the poems dated 1950 and 1861. My earlier examination of her drafting of the published antimilitarist poem "View of the Capital from the Library of Congress" in her diary of 1950 reveals that she chose to use the same artistic method to render both poems about 1950 and 1861. She created "View of the Capitol from the Library of Congress" from diary excerpts just as she had constructed "From Trollope's Journal" from his journal about the Civil War. Moreover, both poems critique U.S. militarism through a discourse of pathology (soldiers' poisoning in the Civil War, 1861; air force impotence in the Cold War and the Korean War, 1950) that also appears in both writers' journals.

Bishop and Trollope intertwine private illness with political malaise in their observations about Washington, D.C. Bishop's "From Trollope's Journal" ties together Trollope's anthrax, Lincoln's ague or fever, the surgeon's sore throat, and the Civil War. The prose and poetry drafts in her diary of 1950, "View of the Capitol from the Library of Congress," "Visits to St. Elizabeths," as well as "From Trollope's Journal" connect the Cold War (and the Korean War, the first official U.S. Cold War military conflict), Pound's hospital confinement, and a national history of political and cultural disease.

Conspicuously absent from this list is any reference to Bishop's health at this time in spite of previously cited evidence that she was very ill. In her diary of 1950 Bishop wrote at the front of the journal that it was her "worst year" so far (Folder 77.4, VC). In addition, she intertwined her developing poem about the nation's military outburst in the Korean War with prose discourse about her personal suffering. The previously discussed journal entry analyzing a highly private upset appears on the same page with the earlier prose excerpt about the imagined "short burst" of the band music. In the next several journal entries written on June 24 and 25, 1950, in Maryland at Dewey's home, Bishop records the title of "View of the Capitol from the Library of Congress" and sketches out the poem in its entirety for the first time, thereby linking her private distress with the nation's.

One has to wonder if her extended absences from her government post in Washington and her frequent long stays in the Maryland countryside did not constitute a strategy of avoidance. Bishop welcomed Dewey's home as a haven away from the escalating government surveillance. While it appears that Bishop's visits to Dewey's were harbors of rest, it is crucial to also note that Dewey was a physicist who worked in defense. So when Bishop described a military-dominated, feminine-coded pastoral world in her poetry drafts, she also seems to have encoded the fact that her so-called haven away from the Cold War was another complicitous center endangered by nuclear politics.

It is difficult to avoid connecting Bishop's declaration at the end of "From Trollope's Journal" that "everyone's sick! The soldiers poison the air" to her estimate that Cold War politics was "poisoning" her entire world—from her public life as poetry consultant to the Library of Congress to her private life at Dewey's Maryland home. Bishop's periodic rescue or retreat from Washington was as compromised as Trollope's medical treatment by the surgeon in "From Trollope's Journal," who is ill himself with "sore throat." Bishop sought care from Dewey who was implicated herself in the very "poisoning" that threatened her.

In addition to this highly personal quasi-(in)visible text of dissent in the poem, the imagery of poisoning and disease suggests a quasi-visible text focused more directly on the quagmire of poetry politics at Yaddo that Bishop faced in her year in Washington. Lowell had used the Cold War rhetoric of disease, comparing Yaddo to a body and calling Ames "a diseased organ, chronically poisoning the whole system." Yet he was the diseased organ himself, charging an innocent woman and rupturing the literary community in a manifestation of his manic-depressive disorder. Bishop also had sought mentoring and protection from Lowell in her poetry career; and his actions had frightened her. Had he caused her to wonder if he would attack her?

Bishop's 1949–50 year in Washington as poetry consultant to the Library of Congress was, then, hardly a year that merits being described as generally silent without further elaboration. She left behind a spasmodic, sporadic record of speech in her journal of 1950 that offers sketches of reticent and ill "versions," but also politically charged and secretive, self-protecting public and private "versions." Bishop did not ignore the fact that the Cold War, as well as the Korean War, was springing up in her "back yard" at the Library of Congress.

As the following conclusion will discuss, she seems to have constructed her long-acknowledged "12 O'Clock News" from the writing associated with her year in Washington that had allowed her to consolidate a vision of death at the hands of Cold War militarized culture rather than the victory it falsely promised. "Desk at Night" of 1950 could have been entitled "to see the end," to use Bishop's memorable line from "Roosters."

Chapter 7 ⟿

CONCLUSION:
"TO SEE THE END"

F rom her apartment in San Francisco, which reminded her fondly and
perhaps ominously of Key West, Bishop deplored the airplanes that
were taking off and returning every night right above her during
the Vietnam conflict (*OA* 503-4). She may have even wondered at times
from her late 1960s home which war the planes were flying in—for she
had heard war planes daily before. She had complained about them during
the Second World War in Key West to Russell and then in the Korean War
in Washington to Frankenberg. Moreover, she had meditated upon their
destructive bombing power in "Roosters," her poetry fragment "V-Day
August 14th, 1945," and "View of the Capitol from the Library of Congress," foregrounding their apocalyptic aftermath, or what it was like "to see
the end."

Bishop had surmised, as we have seen, that the Cold War narrative was
catastrophic from its inception. But "containment," with its policy of foreign intervention in order to protect U.S. interests against Communism,
remained the hegemonic politics of the Cold War. This perspective was
condescending towards such developing nations as Korea and Vietnam as
well as Brazil, where Bishop lived throughout most of the 1950s and to the
mid–1960s. The result was devastating. In Korea, for instance, "the enemy,
wherever located, had not been vanquished despite three years of hellish
destruction" and millions had been killed by the time a decision was made
to install United Nations peacekeeping forces (Engelhardt 62; 65).

In October of 1950, just about the same time that she completed "View
of the Capitol from the Library of Congress," Bishop sent Miller a version
of "Desk at Night" entitled "Little Exercise" from Yaddo and apparently
attempted to place the poem with Katherine White at *The New Yorker*, with

no success (*OA* 430). This early full draft now in Bishop's archives tends to be either ignored or considered only in the history of the much-later version of the poem known as "12 O'Clock News," published in *The New Yorker* in 1973 and immediately regarded as an anti-Vietnam poem, although Bishop never explicitly said it was set there. Indeed one of the poem's most haunting features is the warfront that seems both transcendent and global as well as localized, not surprising since Bishop must have had a sense of war's repetition through the daily presence of the airplanes overhead in San Francisco.

As this narrative has argued, early or abandoned drafts, however, reveal unread, alternative public and private "versions" of Bishop in the time between early World War II and the move to Brazil in the early Cold War during the Korean War that contradict the canonical "versions" of the silent and ill Bishop. They indicate that she chose to wait for more open moments of publication once the poem was rejected rather than abandon the poem completely. Because Bishop thought highly enough of the poem to mail it to Miller and White, it belongs in this multinarrative about her spasmodic and sporadic attempts at speech in a time of strategic dissenting silence.

Apparently both Miller and White did not understand the poem's puzzle about how the various writing tools on Bishop's desk could offer a view of war as much as Bishop had hoped they would by presenting it as a "guess what" poem. Miller urged her to be less cryptic. After thanking Bishop in typescript for her "ode to the desk top," Miller then scribbled in handwriting the date of October 27 with an encouraging note saying she wanted to see more (Folder 12.4, VC). Miller was so excited by the poem's depiction of Bishop's personal desk that she longed to write a poem about her own disarrayed desk.

What Bishop's poetic imagination had created with the quasi-(in)visible objects on her desk is a quasi-(in)visible antiheroic victory culture plot while the Cold War national policymakers attempted to demand that cultural producers recycle the World War II victory narrative to meet the new anti-Communist ideological goals. Like the listener at the air force concert in "View of the Capitol from the Library of Congress," Bishop was not in total thrall to the Cold War call to arms. Her airplane or aerial view in the poem of the bombed scene below focuses on its devastating realities rather than the euphoria of victory, as the poet-narrator highlights the exhausted, frightened unicyclist fleeing his mangled and tossed dead soldier-comrades in the machine-gun nest rather than acting like a World War II hero (Folder 77.5, p. 1, VC).

While in the war poem "Roosters," the narrator-civilian looks outside the window on the allegorical "unwanted" airplane invasion scene in the back yard, in this poem the narrator looks down from an aerial window on the scene after the bombing into the "ash heap" of soldiers to "see the end." Exactly what the narrator is doing here is unclear, in sharp contrast to the awakened narrator at home in "Roosters." Is the narrator a civilian eye-witness? A reporting writer? A military inspector? We realize that the poet is narrating her own desk, which is now viewed as a war zone, but her role in the victory plot is blurred just as the boundaries between civilians and the military broke down in World War II–Cold War culture. We also do not know where the desk is located, but given the timing of the draft of "Desk at Night" it seems likely that it is either the desk at the Library of Congress, her desk of refuge from the Washington warfront at Dewey's farm where nuclear blasting interrupted her writing and the civilian world surrounding the testing sites, or her desk at Yaddo just before or after her appointment at the library.

The narrator's emotional identification with the fallen exhausted unicyclist whose hair is raised with fear from having deserted his dead comrades suggests that the poet-narrator already has begun to understand the meaning of the much later Vietnam-era term "quagmire." The unicyclist has escaped his comrades' fates, but we do not know if he will be able to reach safety between this bombing attack and the next one.

Bishop's preoccupation with death in this 1950 poem also ties in with her view of the inevitable result of the Cold War venture. She treated Washington architecture as "piles of granite," cemetery markers, in her letter to Bell during her year in Washington, portrayed the martial music of the Air Force band with its camouflaged deadly "boom-boom" from the east steps in front of the Capitol in "View of the Capitol from the Library of Congress," and explored the different angles of the diseased Fascist Pound at St. Elizabeth's Hospital. Bishop also focused on this imagery in the World War II–era before this, not surprising given that Millier states that the poem existed in fragment as early as the interwar period of the 1930s as Bishop "recorded a series of transparent dreams that link the tools of her trade, particularly typewriters, with images suggesting war. In one dream, the typewriter keys are a code she must solve" (134). Bishop had explored the "torn bit" of paper in "V-Day August 14th, 1945," the "gray ash-heap" in "Roosters," the sinking ship with "lead in its breast," and the haunting faces in the leaves in "Songs for a Colored Singer."

In addition to this version of the poem, sometime in her year at the Library of Congress or shortly afterwards, Bishop scribbled a sketchy outline of a two-column version of the objects and narration in the poem on the front of an envelope from the Institute of Contemporary Art addressed to her at the Library of Congress. It is not clear whether this sketch came before the early conventional unified plot version of "Desk at Night" entitled "Little Exercise" sent to Miller and White or was simply another draft of it.

Bishop mapped out the handwritten sketch between her name and address and the art institute's address, bringing together through this juxtaposition the visual imagery and verbal imagery that play such a major intertwined role in the poem. After sketching the choices of "Desk & Moonlight" or "The Desk at Night" for the title, the poet lists most of the objects, with slight variations in wording, that eventually appear much later in "12 O'Clock News": the typewriter, piles of manuscript, typed sheet, envelopes, ink-bottle, typewriter eraser, and ash tray with cigarette butts. This two-column format not only sets up tension as it did in "View of the Capitol from the Library of Congress." It also shows that Bishop has decided to transform her (in)visible double texts of visual objects and narration into visible texts barely held together by dashes (Folder 77.5, p. 1, VC).

The narrator has disappeared behind the apparently objective, but camouflaged and subjective, arrangement of the list. Any sense of personal connection also has begun to break down. We do not know precisely when Bishop began to consider traveling outside of North America again, but the kind of distancing that occurs in "Desk at Night" also was occurring in her private life.

In 1951 she decided to move in with Lota de Macedo Soares in Brazil, carrying with her a skeptical perspective of the U.S. Cold War. She told U.T. and Joseph Summers in a letter on September 17, 1952, that she found it much easier to live as she wanted in Brazil and was excited about the prospect of Adlai Stevenson winning the White House, revealing her concerns about the limitations placed upon her in the U.S. (*OA* 247). In the 1956 Presidential election, Bishop deplored the fact that Moore had appeared on a list of "Egg-Heads for Eisenhower" to Bell in a December 10, 1956, letter, finding the thought of Eisenhower as president impossible (Folder 24.6 VC).

Bishop's concerns about Eisenhower were warranted, given her social and cultural perspectives. In April of 1953, for example, he issued an executive order authorizing the most comprehensive investigation of the loyalty of federal employees of the United States in history. This decision dramatically extended the battle against Communist subversives within the country led by HUAC and Senator Joseph McCarthy. By that December, his Secretary of State John Foster Dulles had completed most of the nation's aggressive Cold War foreign policy blueprint called "containment," which called for a policy of "massive retaliation" involving nuclear stock-piling and aggressive military intervention abroad.

The military politics of "containment" also intervened in the selection of the poetry chair that Bishop had held at the Library of Congress. William Carlos Williams was appointed in 1952 but did not serve because he was falsely accused of being a Communist. The post remained vacant until 1956. In a letter to Moore on October 30, 1954, Bishop expressed her horror at Williams's plight and said that she should have resigned from the library fellows to which she belonged, which would have been considered a gesture of protest about the situation (*OA* 299-300).

Although Bishop had hoped to escape the Cold War by living outside of the United States, she found that it followed her to Brazil. She wrote Moore on August 17, 1954, deploring the "McCarthy-y" behavior of the U.S. ambassador to Brazil during Robert Frost's visit. She reported that she was upset about the fact that he sat with an unlit cigar between Frost and Frost's daughter and behaved rudely (*OA* 297). Later, in a March 30, 1959, letter to Bell, she said that she hoped that, if a woman ambassador were appointed to Brazil, someone would explain to her that the embassy here underestimates Brazilian intellectuals and earns their scorn. She pointed out that the embassy seemed unduly excited when it learned that Lowell, who visited Brazil, had been jailed in the United States during the Second World War as a conscientious objector (Folder 24.9, VC).

Bishop found herself wedged precariously between U.S. Cold War mil-itarism and Brazilian militarism. Periodic waves of anti-Americanism often affected her (*OA* 229). Two letters to Bell in 1961 indicate exactly how precarious Bishop's positioning really was. On one hand, she was appalled when she was working on her *Time-Life* book on Brazil and they asked her if she had been a Communist. Bishop told Bell that probably some "infant" editor had seen one of her poems in *Partisan Review* and the name terrified them. Then she added that they were behaving exactly as the embassy did in Brazil (*OA* 399).

On the other hand, she found herself caught up in the volatile world of internal Brazilian politics because of Soares's alliance with Carlos Lacerda. In a September 2, 1961, letter to Bell, she said that she was in her studio in the country with a .22 at her side (Folder 24.11 VC). So she had not escaped military conflict at all. Indeed, she was now an armed civilian her-self in the increasingly blurred boundaries between civilians and the mili-tary in Brazil.

When a military dictatorship seized power in Brazil in the 1960s,

Bishop began searching for a way to leave the scene of conflict again and found it in a job offer from the University of Washington in 1966 just as "containment" was being challenged by the growing public response to the Vietnam conflict. She hoped that Soares would join her in the United States. But this did not occur. When a very ill Soares visited her in New York in 1967, Soares committed suicide.

Bishop's own scorn of the "Ugly American" attitude of the U.S. Cold War policy informs her three major poems depicting her arrival in Brazil. In "Arrival at Santos" in January 1952, the poem's narrator distances and flattens out everything about Brazil, describing the coast as "a coast"; the harbor as "a harbor," a common technique in victory culture. As Engelhardt points out, the "other" side always was held "at a distance" to forestall identification with their plight (38-46). Moreover, the narrator fails to recognize that Brazil is a nation—calling its flag a rag because there had been no thought about there being a flag, currency, coinage, or another language. In short, the narrator has had no interest in the realities of another nation and culture. Indeed, the narrator sounds like Henry Kissinger describing North Vietnam as a "little fourth rate power" (Engelhardt 206).

The companion poem "Brazil, January 1, 1502" grounds this victory culture narrator within the history of European colonialism, foregrounding the fact that this Cold War storyteller is simply another version of, or repetition of, many narrators in a long ongoing history of colonial imperialism and militarism. The narrator reveals a desire to be part of this history in the opening lines, conjecturing that nature must have greeted them just as it is greeting us in an attempt to authorize its own narration by its historical common ground with earlier "arrivals." The anxieties of the storyteller in "Arrival at Santos"—that the tourist's immodest demands cannot be met—belong to a long history of anxieties over whether "an old dream of wealth and luxury" can be satisfied by a new colonial possession. Indeed, the 1950s Cold War narrator is linked directly to the Portuguese conquerors who used a Mass to authorize their desire to plunder the native women for their own pleasure and gain. But the women evade their grasp just as the powerful feminized trees in "View of the Capitol from the Library of Congress" apparently block the military music.

The third poem about Bishop's arrival in Brazil entitled "Questions of Travel" continues to foreground the blighted ethnocentric vision of the narrator. Immediately following the native women's resistance and evasion of the "imperial" gaze of colonial conquest, the narrator in this poem denigrates the landscape helping to shield them. We are told, for instance, that the country has too many waterfalls as the narrator continues to express anxiety about the (im)possibility of mapping and controlling all within his or her field of vision.

In all three poems the colonial narrator attempts to exert one dominant controlling viewpoint by offering a primitivized and romanticized vision of the landscape and native women. The Brazilian world is portrayed as a mysterious or elusive Eden that resists any interpretation and therefore remains an eternal object of desire. But this fascination is a matter of power and control; for imperial gazers need to transform this "other" into themselves just as the United States desired to Americanize other nations in its efforts at global domination. While we generally think of the Cold War's mistakes with underestimating and misinterpreting Korea and Vietnam, Bishop would have insisted that Brazil be added to this list.

By "12 O'Clock News," the Vietnam conflict's military-political discourse of quagmire dominates the poem. The news commentator-narrator in the poem is clearly aligned with the imperialistic Cold War ideology. The newscaster denigrates the landscape, treating it as an "inferior" piece of real estate with its poor quality soil, "crude" communication, and nonexistent "industrialization" just as Vietnam policymakers degraded Vietnam as a hopeless, devalued "quagmire." Then to cope with the growing "quagmire," the official war discourse turned Vietnam into the aggressor, "not only transferring agency for all negative action to the land, but instantly devaluing it" (199). Seeing Vietnam as a quagmire was one way "in which Americans attempted to distance themselves from the war's reality. It was part of a language of self-deception and cover-up" (200).

The dead soldiers are not seen as human beings but as heaps in contorted positions. Moreover, their deaths are blamed not on their enemy. The narrator explains that they died because they wore the wrong kind of uniforms, uniforms designed for "winter warfare" and not for the plain, a signal that they were foolish to have trusted their "childish," "hopelessly impractical," and "sadly corrupt" officers and planners. Moreover, they are responsible for their deaths "in their present historical state of superstition and helplessness."

The fallen male unicyclist frightened about deserting his dead comrades in "Desk at Night" has been transformed into a dead unicyclist-courier in "12 O'Clock News." The newscaster treats him as an anthropological curiosity or museum specimen representing an extinct people: "Alive, he would have been small, but undoubtedly proud and erect, with the thick, bristling black hair typical of the indigenes" (*CP* 175). The unicyclist is no longer definitely connected to the soldiers as though he might be a civilian casualty, exactly Bishop's anxiety with the blurring of boundaries between civilians and the military.

It is the two-column format of the poem that discredits the news commentator and the Cold War rhetoric of quagmire rather than the country or the dead soldiers and unicyclist-courier. No clear, logical relationship exists between the writer's tools and the narrative description other than the colonial Cold War worldview imposed on them by the Cold War-invested and infested narrator. The placement of the tools in the left column implies that they are the points of origination for the war discourse.

While the writing tools quite visibly belong to the 12 o'clock news show and, most likely, the newscaster, the narrator's diseased imperial "eye" and discourse remind one very appropriately of the three disturbing Cold War narrators in Bishop's poems about arriving in midcentury Brazil as well as her condemnation of Eisenhower in the poem "From Trollope's Journal." As the 1950s versions of "12 O'Clock News" reveal, all of the poems are tied to Bishop's personal desk at the origination point of the path to the Vietnam conflict—the Korean War. So beneath the visible reporting tools of the news desk and the quasi-visible Brazilian travel guide's desk set are the quasi-(in)visible literary implements of the civilian poet whose desk was being transformed into a war zone with the Cold War "containment" culture and the specific commitment of troops to the Korean War. Already Bishop could "see the end" in this war with its inability to separate the military from the civilian population through her long picture window looking at the Capitol from her poetry consultancy desk (Engelhardt 62). By "12 O'Clock News" she could see on her television screen where this World War II–Cold War victory culture had led.

NOTES ⌐

Chapter 1

1. See Brogan's "Elizabeth Bishop: Perversity as Voice"; Edelman's "The Geography of Gender: Elizabeth Bishop's 'In the Waiting Room'"; Harrison's *Elizabeth Bishop's Poetics of Intimacy*; Oktenberg's review of Lombardi's edited collection, *Elizabeth Bishop: The Geography of Gender*, in *The Women's Review of Books*; Page's "Off-Beat Claves, Oblique Realities: The Key West Notebooks of Elizabeth Bishop"; and Rich's "The Eye of the Outsider: The Poetry of Elizabeth Bishop."
2. Barry, Richard Flynn, Fountain, David Jarraway, Page, and Travisano are important voices on this subject.
3. See Stephanie Coontz's *The Way We Never Were*, Maureen Honey's *Rosie the Riveter*, and Elaine Tyler May's *Homeward Bound* for an excellent overview of this subject.
4. See Terry Castle's *The Apparitional Lesbian* for her discussion of Garbo. See also Dinitia Smith's more recent "Letters Push Garbo Slightly Into View" about Garbo's debated ambiguous sexuality and Mercedes de Acosta's alleged romance with her. She states that no concrete evidence of a sexual relationship between the two women exists.
5. I thank Steven Axelrod for suggesting the political advantage of Bishop's position at this time.

Chapter 2

1. It is not surprising to find the "high culture" Bishop sharing a page in the magazine with Wayne's "pop" personification of the heroic American. Such provocative editorializing was a trademark of the magazine's editor at the time, Tina Brown. Brown said that juxtaposition and positioning were cru-

cial in the composition of the magazine in a television interview on *The Charlie Rose Show,* January 13, 1998.

2. I thank George Monteiro for drawing this film to my attention. For further discussion of how plays, films, and teleplays responded to the HUAC hearings, see Brenda Murphy's *Congressional Theatre.*

3. See "John Wayne's Body," *The New Yorker,* August 19, 1996, pp. 39-49. The insert "Easel by Elizabeth Bishop" features the watercolor of a sleeping woman and the poems "Foreign-Domestic" and "A Lovely Finish . . ." on pp. 46-47. William Benton, editor of the published collection of her art entitled *Exchanging Hats: Paintings,* identifies the woman in "Sleeping Figure" as most likely Louise Crane, Bishop's lifelong friend with whom she traveled and lived in Key West during the 1930s and 1940s (10).

4. This field of scholarship is too vast to overview even briefly. I refer the reader to such examples of major works on culture, gender, and war as Miriam Cooke's edited collection *Gendering War Talk;* Helen Cooper's edited collection *Arms and the Woman;* Cynthia Enloe's *Does Khaki Become You? The Militarization of Women's Lives* and "Feminists Thinking About War, Militarism and Peace" in *Analyzing Gender;* Jean Bethke Elshtain's *Women and War;* Margaret and Patrice Higonnet's edited collection *Behind the Lines;* Sharon Macdonald, Pat Holden, and Shirley Basingstoke's *Images of Women in Peace and War;* Judith Hicks Stiehm's edited issue on women and men's wars in the *Women's Studies International Forum,* 1982; Susan Schweik's *A Gulf So Deeply Cut;* Carol Berkin and Clara Lovett's edited *Women, War and Revolution;* bell hooks's "Feminism and Militarism" in her *Talking Back;* Micaela Di Leonardo's "Morals, Mothers, and Militarism: Antimilitarism and Feminist Theory"; Nancy Huston's "The Matrix of War: Mothers and Heroes"; Sara Ruddick's *Maternal Thinking: Towards a Politics of Peace;* Carol Cohn's "Sex and Death in the Rational World of Defense Intellectuals"; Claire Tylee's *The Great War and Women's Consciousness;* Susan Hartmann's *The Home Front and Beyond;* and D'Ann Campbell's *Women at War in America.*

5. See Lillian Faderman's *Odd Girls & Twilight Lovers* for more detail on the history and problems of lesbians in this era. See also Lisa Meyer's *Creating G.I. Jane* for a relevant examination of female sexuality and race in the military.

6. Because of our culture's traditional as well as current training of readers to approach texts as heterosexually focused, establishing a general reading practice for Bishop based on the hierarchy of universalized heterosexual text and lesbian subtext as Dickie does is useful (85). I do not wish, however, to overlook the potential for coequal interrelated texts of importance even if readers are not trained to see them this way yet.

7. Personal conversation with Alice Quinn, October 11, 1997. Also see *The Elizabeth Bishop Society Bulletin,* Summer 1996, p. 4. For Benton details, see p. 10.

8. See Betsy Erkkila's "Bishop, Modernism and the Left"; John Palattella's "'That Sense of Constant Readjustment': The Great Depression and the

Provisional Politics of Elizabeth Bishop's *North & South*"; and Celeste
Goodridge's "Elizabeth Bishop and Wallace Stevens: Sustaining the Eye/I" to
obtain more comprehensive and competing treatments of Bishop in the
1930s scene.

9. See discussions of cultural hegemony in T. J. Jackson Lears's "The Concept
   of Cultural Hegemony: Problems and Possibilities," *The American Historical
   Review* 90, no. 3 (1985), pp. 567-593; Robert Bocock's *Hegemony;* and
   Joseph Femia's *Gramsci's Political Thought*.
10. I thank Steven Axelrod for encouraging me to clarify the national multi-
    narratives.

Chapter 3

1. Hereafter *One Art* is abbreviated as *OA*.
2. Bishop was made aware of the Vatican's war politics by Lowell, who wrote
   her in a letter of June 19, 1967 (Vassar Archives) about an invitation to adapt
   Rolf Hochhuth's 1963 play *The Deputy* with Lillian Hellman. This play
   marked the beginning of the debate about the Vatican's politics. Lowell told
   Bishop that he was not interested in any anti-Catholic diatribe but felt that
   the play deserved a hearing. Lowell did not adapt the play. For one of the
   most recent texts on the Vatican's World War II politics, see John Cornwell's
   Hitler's Pope: The Secret History of Pius XII (1999). For a summary of Pope
   John Paul II's apology for the errors of the Church for over two thousand
   years and its relationship to the Vatican during the Second World War, see
   "Excerpts from the Apology by the Pope and Cardinals" in the March 13,
   2000, issue of *The New York Times,* A10.
3. Hereafter the abbreviation VC will designate Vassar College.
4. Hereafter the abbreviation *CP* will designate *The Complete Poems*.
5. I wish to thank Susan Gubar for bringing this poem to my attention.
6. See Schweik's *A Gulf So Deeply Cut* for an excellent related overview of
   Millay's World War II - era poetry.
7. Cuthbert published Millay's radio script in her book *Adventure in Radio* in
   1945, also including with it scripts by MacLeish, Arch Oboler, Edward R.
   Murrow, Edgar Bergen, Stephen Vincent Benet, George Hicks, Wright
   Bryan, and Roy Porter. This book is available at the John Hay Library,
   Brown University.
8. See Schweik for a comprehensive treatment of this Second World War
   writing.
9. It is not clear how well known her artistic work was among her friends and
   acquaintances at this time.
10. See Steven Axelrod's essay "Was Elizabeth Bishop a Racist?" for an impor-
    tant reading of "Cootchie." I agree with his conclusion that she reproduces
    her era's racist representations alongside her own attempts at empathy.

Chapter 4

1. The positioning of the "frontier" and the "pastoral" in U.S. history is a sub-field of study. Useful works of introduction to the field include Richard Slotkin's *Gunfighter Nation: The Myth of the Frontier in Twentieth-Century America*, Annette Kolodny's *The Lay of the Land,* Henry Nash Smith's *Virgin Land,* Leo Marx's *The Machine in the Garden,* and R. W. B. Lewis's *The American Adam.*

2. I thank Travisano for pointing out Bishop's effective use of "we" and "our" in the poem.

3. I thank Travisano for pointing out the way that literature and film noir exposed previously sanitized war imagery very early.

4. See my essay, "Frank O'Hara and Music as Ethnography: The Example of 'The Day Lady Died'" for a relevant reading of this poem.

5. I thank Ruth Oppenheim, who left Germany shortly after Kristallnacht with her family, for recalling the treatment of targeted groups, including homosexuals, in a conversation on September 30, 1998. For one of the most recent texts on Jewish homosexuality in Nazi Germany, see Gad Beck's *An Underground Life: The Memoirs of a Gay Jew in Nazi Berlin.*

Chapter 5

1. I thank Axelrod for his insight into Kennan's complexity.

2. Kennan's major diplomatic policy statements appear in *Memoirs 1925-1950, Memoirs 1950-1963,* and *Nuclear Delusion.*

3. The demobilization collaboration between the white women's press and the national government is well documented, although scant attention has been paid to the depiction of women poets. See, for example, Betty Friedan's *The Feminine Mystique,* Susan Hartmann's *The Home Front and Beyond,* Maureen Honey's *Creating Rosie the Riveter,* and Elaine Tyler May's *Homeward Bound.*

4. The archive files at Vassar College document the relationship of this four-some at length.

5. For more information about the friendships of Bishop, Jarrell, and Lowell as well as Berryman, see Travisano's *Midcentury Quartet.*

6. See Boxwell for this description of my essay, "Washington, D.C., 1949-1950: Bishop on WWII & the Cold War." I thank him for his apt characterization.

Chapter 6

1. See my essay "Cold War 1950: Elizabeth Bishop and Sylvia Plath" for a more complete reading of this poem. Plath uses the device of three women's voices again much later in a more comprehensive exploration of Cold War culture in *Three Women.*

2. Dickie's chapters four and five in *Stein, Bishop, Rich* treat Bishop's lyrics of lesbian love and war generally in very useful ways but do not argue that they may be interrelated during the year in Washington.

3. For related readings of "View of the Capitol from the Library of Congress," "From Trollope's Journal," and the journal of 1950, see my "Bishop's Washington, D.C.: Sites of Gore and Glory," "Cold War 1950: Elizabeth Bishop and Sylvia Plath," and "Washington, D.C., 1949–950: Bishop on WWII & the Cold War."

4. My reading has benefited from conversations with John Gonzales, who wrote on this poem for my graduate seminar in 1994.

5. Several of these postcards can be seen in the Vassar archives.

6. I wish to thank Travisano for encouraging me to continue interrogating this aspect of the poem.

7. The use of the nursery rhyme schema here seems related to Plath's reliance upon it as well in "Daddy." Both poets castigate the Fascist "father" within an infantile poetry form.

BIBLIOGRAPHY

Althusser, Louis. *For Marx*. London: New Left Books, 1977.

Anderson, Benedict. *Imagined Communities: Reflections on the Origin and Spread of Nationalism*. 2nd ed. London: Verso, 1991.

Anthias, Floya, and Nira Yuval-Davis, ed. *Women, Nation, State*. London: Macmillan, 1989.

Axelrod, Steven. "Lowell and the Cold War." *New England Quarterly* (September 1999): 339–61.

———. "The Middle Generation and WWII: Jarrell, Shapiro, Brooks, Bishop, Lowell." *WLA: War, Literature & the Arts*. 11.1 (Spring/Summer 1999): 1–41.

———. "Was Elizabeth Bishop a Racist?" In *'In Worcester, Massachusetts': Essays on Elizabeth Bishop*, ed. Laura Menides and Angela Dorenkamp. New York: Peter Lang, 1999.

Barry, Sandra, Gwendolyn Davies, and Peter Sanger, ed. *Division of the Heart: Elizabeth Bishop's Art of Place and Memory*. Wolfville, Nova Scotia: Gaspereau Press, 2000.

———. "Elizabeth Bishop and World War I." *WLA: War, Literature & the Arts* 11.1 (Spring/Summer 1999): 93–110.

———. *Elizabeth Bishop: An Archival Guide to Her Life in Nova Scotia*. Nova Scotia: The Elizabeth Bishop Society of Nova Scotia, 1996.

———. "Invisible Threads and Individual Rubatos: Migration in Elizabeth Bishop's Life and Work" In *'In Worcester, Massachusetts': Essays on Elizabeth Bishop*, ed. Laura Menides and Angela Dorenkamp. New York: Peter Lang, 1999.

Bates, Milton. *The Wars We Took to Vietnam*. Berkeley: University of California Press, 1996.

Beck, Gad. *An Underground Life: The Memoirs of a Gay Jew in Nazi Berlin*. Madison: University of Wisconsin Press, 1999.

Bérubé, Alan. *Coming Out Under Fire: The History of Gay Men and Women in World War Two*. New York: Free Press-Macmillan, 1990.

Bhaba, Homi. *Nation and Narration*. New York: Routledge, 1991.

Bishop, Elizabeth. Bishop Archive. Vassar College Library.

———. *Elizabeth Bishop: The Collected Prose*. New York: Farrar, Straus, Giroux, 1984.

———. *Elizabeth Bishop: The Complete Poems, 1927-1979*. New York: Farrar, Straus, Giroux, 1983.

———. *Exchanging Hats*. Artwork selected, edited, and introduced by William Benton. New York: Farrar, Straus, Giroux, 1996.

———. "Foreign-Domestic." *The New Yorker,* August 19, 1996: 47.

———. "A Lovely Finish." *The New Yorker,* August 19, 1996: 47.

———. *One Art*. Letters selected and edited by Robert Giroux. New York: Farrar, Straus, Giroux, 1994.

Blasing, Mutlu. *Politics and Form in Postmodern Poetry: O'Hara, Bishop, Ashbery, and Merrill*. Cambridge: Cambridge University Press, 1995.

Bogan, Louise. Review of *North & South*. *The New Yorker,* October 5, 1946: 113.

Booth, Allyson. *Postcards from the Trenches*. New York: Oxford, 1997.

Bourdieu, Pierre. *The Field of Cultural Production*. New York: Columbia University Press, 1993.

Boxwell, David. "'The Middle Generation' of American Poetry: Wars in the Private and Public Realms." *WLA: War, Literature & the Arts* 11.1 (Spring/Summer 1999): i–iii.

Boyer, Paul. *By the Bomb's Early Light: American Thought and Culture at the Dawn of the Atomic Age*. New York: Pantheon, 1985.

Braw, Monica. *The Atomic Suppressed American Censorship in Occupied Japan*. Armonk, NY: M. E. Sharpe, 1991.

Brogan, Jacqueline Vaught. "Elizabeth Bishop: Perversity as Voice." *American Poetry* 7.2 (Winter 1990): 31–49.

———. "Planets on the Table: From Wallace Stevens and Elizabeth Bishop to Adrienne Rich and June Jordan." *The Wallace Stevens Journal* 19.2 (Fall 1995): 255–278.

Brogan, Kathleen. "Lyric Voice and Sexual Difference in Elizabeth Bishop." In *Writing the Woman Artist,* ed. Suzanne Jones. Charlottesville, Va.: The University Press of Virginia, 1991.

Brown, Tina. Interview. *The Charlie Rose Show.* January 13, 1998.

Butler, Judith. *Gender Trouble: Feminism and the Subversion of Identity*. New York and London: Routledge, 1990.

Castle, Terry. *The Apparitional Lesbian: Female Homosexuality and Modern Culture*. New York: Columbia University Press, 1993.

Conway, Jill Ker. *True North*. New York: Vintage Books, 1994.

Cook, Blanche Weisen. *The Declassified Eisenhower*. New York: Doubleday, 1981.

———. *Eleanor Roosevelt*. Vol. 1. New York: Penguin Books, 1993.

———. *Eleanor Roosevelt*. Vol. 2. New York: Penguin Books, 2000.

Cooke, Miriam, and Angela Woollacott, ed. *Gendering War Talk*. Princeton: Princeton University Press, 1993.

Coontz, Stephanie. *The Way We Never Were: American Families & the Nostalgia Trap.* New York: Basic Books, 1992.

Cornwell, John. *Hitler's Pope: The Secret History of Pius XII.* New York: Viking, 1999.

Costello, Bonnie. *Elizabeth Bishop: Questions of Mastery.* Cambridge: Harvard University Press, 1991.

Cuthbert, Margaret, ed. *Adventure in Radio.* New York: Howell, Soskin Publishers, 1945.

Davidson, Michael. "Postwar Poetry & the Politics of Containment." *American Literary History* 11.1: 25–51.

de Certeau, Michel. *The Practice of Everyday Life.* Trans. Steven Rendall. Berkeley: University of California Press, 1984.

Dickie, Margaret. *Stein, Bishop, Rich: Lyrics of Love, War, & Place.* Chapel Hill: The University of North Carolina Press, 1997.

Dobrzynski, Judith H. "A Peek at Life in an Artists' Retreat." *The New York Times* July 19, 1999: B1, B4.

Donaldson, Scott. *Archibald MacLeish: An American Life.* Boston: Houghton Mifflin, 1992.

Doreski, William. *The Years of Our Friendship: Robert Lowell and Allen Tate.* Jackson: University of Mississippi Press, 1990.

Dubois, W. E. B. Editorial: "World War & the Color Line." *Crisis* November 1914: 28–29.

Edel, Leon, ed. *Edmund Wilson: The Forties.* New York: Harcourt, 1983.

Edelman, Lee. "The Geography of Gender: Elizabeth Bishop's 'In the Waiting Room.'" In *Elizabeth Bishop: The Geography of Gender,* ed. Marilyn May Lombardi, 91–107. Charlottesville: University Press of Virginia, 1993.

————. "Tearooms and Sympathy, or, The Epistemology of the Water Closet." In *Nationalisms and Sexualities,* ed. Andrew Parker, et. al., 263–84. New York: Routledge, 1992.

Electric Light & Power Council. Advertisement. *Time,* May 22, 1950: 6.

Ellis, Sally. "U.S. Poetry Chair Holder Tells How She Courts the Muse." *Boston Post Magazine.* January 18, 1950: 3.

Elshtain, Jean Bethke. *Women and War.* New York: Basic Books, 1987.

Engelhardt, Tom. *The End of Victory Culture: Cold War America and the Disillusionment of a Generation.* New York: Basic Books, 1995.

Enloe, Cynthia. *Does Khaki Become You? The Militarization of Women's Lives.* London: Pluto, 1983.

"Excerpts from the Apology by the Pope and Cardinals." *The New York Times* March 13, 2000: A10.

"Ezra Pound and the Bollingen Award." *The Saturday Review of Literature,* July 2, 1949: 20–21.

Faderman, Lillian. *Odd Girls and Twilight Lovers: A History of Lesbian Life in Twentieth-Century America.* New York: Penguin, 1991.

Farnham, Marynia, and Ferdinand Lundberg. *The Modern Woman: The Lost Sex.* New York: Harper, 1947.

Flanzbaum, Hilene. "Surviving the Marketplace: Robert Lowell and the Sixties." *New England Quarterly* 68 (March 1995): 44-57.

Flynn, Richard. *Randall Jarrell and the Lost World of Childhood.* Athens: University of Georgia Press, 1990.

Foucault, Michel. *Power/Knowledge.* New York: Pantheon, 1980.

Fountain, Gary, and Peter Brazeau. *Remembering Elizabeth Bishop: An Oral Biography.* Amherst: University of Massachusetts Press, 1994.

Friedan, Betty. *The Feminine Mystique.* New York: Dell, 1963.

Fussell, Paul. *The Great War & Modern Memory.* New York: Oxford, 1975.

———. *Wartime.* London: Oxford, 1987.

Gaddis, John Lewis. *Strategies of Containment.* New York: Oxford, 1982.

Gibbs, Christopher. *Silent Majority: Missouri's Resistance to World War I.* Columbia: University of Missouri Press, 1982.

Gilbert, Sandra. "Soldier's Heart: Literary Men, Literary Women, and the Great War." In *Behind the Lines: Gender and the Two World Wars,* ed. Margaret and Patrice Higonnet, 197-226. New Haven: Yale University Press, 1987.

Gilbert, Sandra, and Susan Gubar. *No Man's Land.* Vols. 1 and 2. New Haven: Yale University Press, 1988 and 1989.

Ginder, Richard. "Red Fascism." *Catholic World.* 162 (1946): 491.

"The Golden Years Before the Wars." *Life,* January 2, 1950: 13-28.

Goldensohn, Lorrie. *Elizabeth Bishop: The Biography of a Poetry.* New York: Columbia University Press, 1992.

———. "Randall Jarrell's War." *WLA: War, Literature & the Arts* 11.1 (Spring/Summer 1999): 42-69.

Goodwin, Doris Kearns. *Eleanor and Franklin: The War Years.* New York: Norton, 1995.

Graham, Katharine. *Personal History.* New York: Knopf, 1997.

Gramsci, Antonio. *Selections from Prison Notebooks.* Ed. and trans. Quentin Hoace and Geoffrey Nowell Smith. New York: International, 1971.

Greyhound advertisement. *Time,* May 22, 1950: 8.

Gubar, Susan. "'This is My Rifle, This is My Gun': World War II and the Blitz on Women." In *Behind the Lines: Gender and the Two World Wars,* ed. Margaret and Patrice Higonnet, 227-59. New Haven: Yale University Press, 1987.

Gullace, Nicoletta. "Sexual Violence & Family Honor: British Propaganda & International Law during the First World War." *American Historical Review,* June 1997: 714-747.

———. "White Feathers and Wounded Men: Female Patriotism and the Memory of the Great War." *Journal of British Studies,* April 1997: 177-206.

Hamilton, Ian. *Robert Lowell: A Biography.* New York: Vintage Press, 1982.

Harrison, Victoria. *Elizabeth Bishop's Poetics of Intimacy.* Cambridge: Cambridge University Press, 1993.

Hartmann, Susan. *The Home Front and Beyond.* Boston: Twayne, 1982.

Hein, Laura and Mark Selden, ed. *Living with the Bomb: American and Japanese Cultural Conflicts in the Nuclear Age.* Armonk, NY: M. E. Sharpe, 1991.

Higonnet, Margaret and Patrice. "The Double Helix." In *Behind the Lines: Gender and the Two World Wars,* ed. Margaret and Patrice Higonnet, 1-47. New Haven: Yale University Press, 1987.

————, eds. *Behind the Lines: Gender and the Two World Wars.* New Haven: Yale University Press, 1987.

Hilbish, D. Melissa. "Advancing in Another Direction: The Comic Book and the Korean War." *WLA: War, Literature & the Arts* 11.1 (Spring/Summer 1999): 209-27.

Hillyer, Robert. "Poetry's New Priesthood." *The Saturday Review of Literature,* June 11, 1949: 7-8, 38.

————. "Treason's Strange Fruit/The Case of Ezra Pound and the Bollingen Award. *"The Saturday Review of Literature,* June 11, 1949: 9-11, 28.

Honey, Maureen. *Creating Rosie the Riveter.* Amherst: University of Massachusetts Press, 1984.

Jarraway, David. "'O Canada!': The Spectral Lesbian Poetics of Elizabeth Bishop." *PMLA,* March 1998: 243-57.

Jarrell, Randall. *Poetry and the Age.* New York: Knopf, 1953.

Kaledin, Eugenia. *Mothers and More: American Women in the Fifties.* Boston: Twayne, 1984.

Kazin, Alfred. *New York Jew.* New York: Knopf, 1984.

Keegan, John. *Fields of Battle.* New York: Knopf, 1996.

Keller, Lynn. *Re-making it New: Contemporary American Poetry and the Modernist Tradition.* Cambridge: Cambridge University Press, 1987.

————. "Words Worth a Thousand Postcards: The Bishop/Moore Correspondence." *American Literature* 55: 405-29.

Keller, Lynn, and Cristanne Miller. "Emily Dickinson, Elizabeth Bishop, and the Rewards of Indirection." *The New England Quarterly* Vol. 57, December 1984, 4: 533-53.

Kennan, George P. *Memoirs 1925-1950.* New York: Pantheon, 1984.

————. *Nuclear Delusion.* New York: Pantheon, 1982.

————. "The Sources of Soviet Conduct." *Foreign Affairs,* July 1947: 566-82.

Kozol, Wendy. *Life's America: Family & Nation in Postwar Journalism.* Philadelphia: Temple University Press, 1994.

Kristéva, Julia. "Stabat Mater." *The Kristéva Reader,* ed. Toril Moi. New York: Columbia University Press, 1986. 106-86.

Lakoff, Robin. "Language and Woman's Place." In *The Women & Language Debate: A Sourcebook,* ed. Camille Roman et al. 280-91. New Brunswick: Rutgers University Press, 1994.

Lash, Joseph. *Roosevelt and Churchill, 1939-1941.* New York: Norton, 1976.

"The Laurels." *Time,* April 10, 1950: 36.

LeHand, Marguerite. Letter to Edna St. Vincent Millay. January 2, 1941. Papers of President Franklin D. Roosevelt. Franklin D. Roosevelt Library, Hyde Park, New York.

"A Letter from the Librarian of Congress." *The Saturday Review of Literature,* July 2, 1949: 20-23.

Lombardi, Marilyn May. *The Body and the Song: Elizabeth Bishop's Poetics.* Carbondale: Southern Illinois University Press, 1995.

————, ed. *Elizabeth Bishop: The Geography of Gender.* Charlottesville: University Press of Virginia, 1993.

Longenbach, James. "Elizabeth Bishop and the Story of Postmodernism." *Southern Review.* 28.3 (July 1992): 469-484.

MacKinnon, Janice and Stephen. *Agnes Smedley: The Life and Times of an American Radical.* Berkeley: University of California Press, 1988.

MacLeish, Archibald. *A Time to Speak.* Boston: Houghton Mifflin, 1941.

Margolick, David. *Strange Fruit: Billie Holiday, Café Society, and an Early Cry for Civil Rights.* Philadelphia: Running Press, 2000.

Mariani, Paul. *Lost Puritan: A Life of Robert Lowell.* New York: Norton, 1994.

May, Elaine Tyler. *Homeward Bound: American Families in the Cold War Era.* New York: Basic Books, 1988.

McCabe, Susan. *Elizabeth Bishop: Her Poetics of Loss.* University Park: The Pennsylvania State University Press, 1994.

McGuire, William. *Poetry's Catbird Seat: The Consultantship in Poetry in the English Language at the Library of Congress, 1937-1987.* Washington, D.C.: Library of Congress, 1988.

Menides, Laura, and Angela Dorenkamp, ed. *'In Worcester, Massachusetts': Essays on Elizabeth Bishop.* New York: Peter Lang, 1999.

Mercer, Kobena. "Recoding Narratives of Race & Nation." *The Independent,* January/February 1989: 19-26.

Merrill, James. "Elizabeth Bishop, 1911-1979." In *Elizabeth Bishop and Her Art,* ed. Lloyd Schwartz and Sybil P. Estess, 259-62. Ann Arbor: University of Michigan Press, 1983.

Michel, Sonya. "American Women and the Discourse of the Democratic Family in World War II." In *Behind the Lines: Gender and the Two World Wars,* ed. Margaret and Patrice Higonnet, 154-67. New Haven: Yale University Press, 1987.

Millay, Edna St. Vincent. Margaret Cuthbert and Alice Blinn Collection. Vassar College Library.

————. Four War Poems. *The New York Times Magazine,* October 20, 1940: 12.

————. "Lines Written in Passion and in Deep Concern for England, France and My Own Country." *The New York Times,* June 11, 1940: 10.

————. "Not to Be Spattered by His Blood." *The New York Times Magazine.* January 1, 1942: 10.

————. Telegram to Marguerite LeHand. December 27, 1940. Papers of President Franklin D. Roosevelt. Franklin D. Roosevelt Library, Hyde Park.

————. Telegram to President Franklin D. Roosevelt. December 27, 1940. Papers of President Franklin D. Roosevelt. Franklin D. Roosevelt Library, Hyde Park.

————. "Thanksgiving, 1942." *The New York Times Magazine,* November 22, 1942: 3-5.

Millier, Brett. *Elizabeth Bishop: Life and the Memory of It.* Berkeley: University of California Press, 1993.

————. "The Prodigal: Elizabeth Bishop and Alcohol." *Contemporary Literature,* Spring 1998: 54-76.

Mock, James, and Cedric Larson. *Works That Won the War: The Story of the Committee on Public Information, 1917-1919.* Princeton: Princeton University Press, 1939.

Monteiro, George, ed. *Conversations with Elizabeth Bishop.* Jackson: University Press of Mississippi, 1996.

"More on Pound." *The Saturday Review of Literature,* July 30, 1949: 22

Mosse, George. *Nationalism and Sexuality.* Madison: University of Wisconsin Press, 1985.

Murphy, Brenda. *Congressional Theatre: Dramatizing McCarthyism on Stage, Film, and Television.* Cambridge: Cambridge University Press, 1999.

Muschamp, Herbert. "Beneath the Lawns, Seeds of Discontent." *The New York Times,* November 7, 1999: 51.

Nadel, Alan. *Containment Culture: American Narratives, Postmodernism, and the Atomic Age.* Chapel Hill: Duke University Press, 1996.

"The Nation: The Good War." *Time,* May 29, 1950: 1.

Oktenberg, Adrian. Review of Lombardi, *Elizabeth Bishop: The Geography of Gender.* In *The Women's Review of Books* 11 (July 1994): 28-29.

"Our Country and Our Culture." *Partisan Review* 19 (May-June 1952).

Owen, Wilfred. *Wilfred Owen: Collected Letters,* ed. Harold Owen and John Bell. Oxford: Oxford University Press, 1967.

Palattella, John. "That Sense of Constant Readjustment: The Great Depression and the Provisional Politics of Elzabeth Bishop's *North 9 South.*" *Contemporary Literature* 31.1 (Spring 1993): 18-43.

Pareles, Jon, Neil Strauss, Ben Ratliff, and Ann Powers. "Albums as Mileposts In a Musical Center." *The New York Times,* January 3, 2000: B1, B5.

Parker, Andrew, Mary Russo, Doris Sommer, and Patricia Yaeger, ed. *Nationalisms and Sexualities.* New York: Routledge, 1992.

Plath, Sylvia. "Bitter Strawberries." *Christian Science Monitor,* August 11, 1950: 17.

"A Prepared Attack." *The Nation,* December 17, 1949: 598-99.

Quinn, Alice. "Easel by Elizabeth Bishop." *The New Yorker,* August 19, 1996: 46-47.

Rich, Adrienne. "The Eye of the Outsider: The Poetry of Elizabeth Bishop." In *Blood, Bread & Poetry: Selected Prose, 1979-1985.* New York: Norton, 1986.

Roeder, George H., Jr. *The Censored War: American Visual Experience during World War Two.* New Haven: Yale University Press, 1993.

Roman, Camille. "Bishop at Orono, Maine: 'American Poetry in the 1950s' Conference." *The Elizabeth Bishop Bulletin* 5 (Summer 1996): 2.

———. "Bishop's Washington, D.C.: Sites of Gore and Glory." In *Division of the Heart: Elizabeth Bishop's Art of Place and Memory*, ed. Sandra Barry, Gwendolyn Davies, and Peter Sanger. Wolfville, Nova Scotia: Gaspereau Press, 2000.

———. "Cold War 1950: Elizabeth Bishop and Sylvia Plath." In *'In Worcester, Massachusetts': Essays on Elizabeth Bishop*, ed. Laura Menides and Angela Dorenkamp. New York: Peter Lang, 1999.

———. "Frank O'Hara and Music as Ethnography: The Example of 'The Day Lady Died.'" *Yearbook of Interdisciplinary Studies in the Fine Arts* (3) 1992: 15-33.

———. "Washington, D.C., 1949-1950: Bishop on WWII & the Cold War." *WLA: War, Literature & the Arts* 11.1 (Spring/Summer 1999): 125-148.

Roman, Camille, Suzanne Juhasz, and Cristanne Miller, ed. *The Women & Language Debate: A Sourcebook*. New Brunswick: Rutgers University Press, 1994; NetLibrary.com: 1999.

Rupp, Leila. *Mobilizing Women for War: German and American Propaganda, 1939-1945*. Princeton: Princeton University Press, 1978.

"'The Saturday Review' Unfair to Literature." *The Nation*, December 17, 1949: 598.

Savage, William. *Comic Books and America, 1945-1954*. Norman: University of Oklahoma Press, 1990.

Scarry, Elaine. "Injury and the Structure of War." *Representations* 10 (1985): 1-51.

Schlesinger, Arthur, Jr. *The Vital Center: The Politics of Freedom*. Cambridge: Riverside Press, 1962.

Schwartz, Lloyd, and Sybil P. Estess. *Elizabeth Bishop and Her Art*. Ann Arbor: The University of Michigan, 1983.

Schweik, Susan. *A Gulf So Deeply Cut: American Women Poets and the Second World War*. Madison: University of Wisconsin Press, 1991.

Scott, Winfield Townley. "Millay Collected." *Poetry* 63 (March 1944): 335.

Seeing Red: Stories of American Communists. Dir. Julia Reichert and James Klein. Heartland Productions, 1984.

Smith, Dinitia. "Cathedral Bars Ezra Pound From Its Poets' Corner." *The New York Times*, October 23, 1999: A17, A20.

———. "Letters Push Garbo Slightly Into View." *The New York Times*, April 18, 2000: B3.

Smith, Paul. *Discerning the Subject*. Minneapolis: University of Minnesota Press, 1988.

Spiegelman, Warren. "Elizabeth Bishop's 'Natural Heroism.'" *Centennial Review* 22: 28-44.

Spillers, Hortense. "Mama's Baby, Papa's Maybe: An American Grammar Book." In *The Women & Language Debate: A Sourcebook*, ed. Camille Roman et. al., 56-77. New Brunswick: Rutgers University Press, 1994.

"SRL: Unfair to Literature?" *The Saturday Review of Literature*, December 31, 1949: 22.

Stein, Gertrude. *Everybody's Autobiography.* Rpt. New York: Vintage, 1973.

Stimpson, Catherine. "Gertrude Stein and the Lesbian Lie." In *American Women's Autobiography: Fea(s)ts of Memory,* ed. Margo Culley. 152-66. Madison: University of Wisconsin Press, 1992.

Taber, Gladys. "Poet's Kitchen." *Ladies' Home Journal,* February 1949: 56-57; 185.

Thompson, Dorothy. "The Woman Poet." *Ladies' Home Journal,* January 1951: 11-12.

Travisano, Thomas. "Bishop's Shadow-Canon Expands: Two Poems, Watercolor in *New Yorker.*" *The Elizabeth Bishop Bulletin* 5 (Summer 1996): 4.

————. *Elizabeth Bishop: Her Artistic Development.* Charlottesville: University Press of Virginia, 1988.

————. "The Elizabeth Bishop Phenomenon." In *Gendered Modernisms: American Women Poets and Their Readers.* ed. Margaret Dickie and Thomas Travisano. Philadelphia: University of Pennsylvania Press, 1996.

————. *Midcentury Quartet: Bishop, Lowell, Jarrell, Berryman and the Making of a Postmodern Aesthetic.* Charlottesville: University Press of Virginia, 1999.

Trilling, Diana. *We Must March, My Darlings: A Critical Decade.* New York: Harcourt Brace Jovanovich, 1971.

Trollope, Anthony. *North America.* Philadelphia: Lippincott, 1862.

van Wienen, Mark. *Partisans & Poets: The Political Work of American Poetry in the Great War.* Cambridge: Cambridge University Press, 1997.

von Hallberg, Robert. *American Poetry and Culture 1945-1980.* Cambridge: Harvard University Press, 1985.

Walker, Cheryl. "Antimodern, Modern, and Postmodern Millay: Contexts of Revaluation." In *Gendered Modernisms: American Women Poets and Their Readers,* ed. Margaret Dickie and Thomas Travisano, 170-88. Philadelphia: University of Pennsylvania Press, 1996.

Westbrook, Robert. "'I Want a Girl, Just like the Girl that Married Harry James': American Women & the Problem of Political Obligation in World War II." *American Quarterly* December 1990: 587-614.

Whitfield, Stephen J. *The Culture of the Cold War.* Baltimore: The Johns Hopkins University Press, 1991.

Wilbur, Richard. *Responses: Prose Pieces, 1953-1976.* New York: Norton, 1976.

Wills, Garry. "John Wayne's Body." *The New Yorker,* August 19, 1996: 39-49.

Woolf, Virginia. *Three Guineas.* 1915. Rpt. New York: Harcourt Brace Javonovich, 1948.

INDEX ➝

Hillyer, Robert, 106, 159
Hitler, Adolf, 28–30, 33–4
Hochhuth, Rolf, 151 n. 2
Holden, Pat, 150 n. 4
Holiday, Billie, 18, 44, 49, 70–8, 80,
    106, 120, 152 n. 4. *Work:* "Strange
    Fruit," 75, 106.
Hollywood blacklisting, 12, 87
Holocaust, 9, 291; and Jewish refugees,
    34, 67; and Kristallnacht, 34
Homosexuality, 2, 7
Honey, Maureen, 85, 149 n. 3, 152 ch.
    5, n. 3, 159
Hook, Sidney, 88, 104
hooks, bell, 150 n. 4
Hoover, Herbert, 19
Hoover, J. Edgar, 24, 82–4, 86,
    137
Houghton–Mifflin, 50, 120
House Committee on Un–American
    Activities (HUAC), 12, 30, 86,
    118, 124, 144
Howe, Irving, 88
Hughes, Langston, 8
Humphries, Rolfe, 30
Hurst, Fannie, 100
Huston, Nancy, 150 n. 4
Hutchens, John, 48
Huxley, Aldous, 47

Jackson, Shirley, 100
James, Harry, 38
James, Henry, 95
Jarraway, David, 149 n. 2, 159
Jarrell, Randall, 2, 36, 63, 81, 89, 97–8,
    100, 103, 108, 110, 119, 126, 159.
    Works: "Burning of the Letters,"
    36, "Eighth Air Force," 36,
    "Losses," 36
John Paul II, 151 n. 2
John Reed Club, 33
"John Wayne's Body," 12–16 passim
Jones, Suzanne, 156
Juhasz, Suzanne, 162

Kaledin, Eugenia, 100, 159
Kazin, Alfred, 88, 103, 105, 117,
    159
Keegan, John, 36, 159
Kees, Weldon, 125, 131, 133
Keller, Lynn, 4, 49, 68, 159
Kennan, George, 24, 80, 82, 86–7, 152
    ch. 5, n. 2, 159
Kennedy, President John, 137
Kerr, Jean, 100
Key West, 3, 6–7, 12, 18, 27–28, 33,
    135, 140–1
Khrushchev, Nikita S., 90
King, MacKenzie, 45
Kirkpatrick, Ralph, 77
Kissinger, Secretary of State Henry, 13,
    146
Kolodny, Annette, 152 n. 1
Korean War, 1–2, 6, 120–2, 135,
    139–42
Kozol, Wendy, 24, 159
Kristeva, Julia, 72, 159
Kumin, Maxine, 97

Lacerda, Carlos, 145
The Ladies' Home Journal, 9, 89–94, 100
Lakoff, Robin, 129, 159
Larson, Cedric, 23, 161
Lash, Joseph, 34, 159
Lears, T. J. Jackson, 151 ch. 2, n. 9
LeHand, Marguerite (Missy), 38,
    160
Lewis, R. W. B., 152 ch. 4, n. 1
Levertov, Denise, 5, 100
Library of Congress, 1–3, 9
Life, 24, 38, 45, 118, 158
Lincoln, Abraham, 118, 134, 138–9
Lombardi, Marilyn May, 3, 15, 128,
    149 n. 1, 160
Longenbach, James, 160
Look, 38
Lorde, Audre, 5, 100
Lovett, Clara, 150 n. 4
Lowell, Robert, 5, 17, 81, 100, 104–5,